PRAISE FOR *FALLING HOME*

"So many of us go through life fearing hardship, because we worry that a tough blow would shatter us. Through evocative prose and deeply personal stories, Hallie Lord shows us that we may very well be shattered—but that shattering is a good thing, as it reveals the true power and grace that was hidden within us all along."

—Jennifer Fulwiler, author of *Your Blue Flame*

"If our world has any hope, it lies in our ability to be vulnerable in sharing our stories while having faith that there's a purpose to our darkness. In *Falling Home*, Hallie Lord beautifully shows us how to do both, and leaves us filled with hope no matter where in life we might find ourselves."

—Tommy Tighe, author of *#blessedmother* and host of *Saint Dymphna's Playbook* podcast

"*Falling Home* is a book I immediately fell in love with. Hallie's warmth, joy, and fantastic storytelling emanate from its pages. She inspired me to want to sit in her living room, listen to her stories, hear her laughter, and be at home in her peace. She sparked a remembrance of God's pursuit of my heart, day in and day out. She invited me into a deeper and more meaningful relationship with Him, to remember that He is my forever dwelling place, and that He desires a home in my heart. This book offers insights I needed, and I know readers will feel the same."

—Jenna Guizar, founder of Blessed is She

"Good writing is about showing, not telling. The same can be said of Christianity. In *Falling Home*, Hallie Lord shows her readers what Christian faith looks like in a profoundly human, humble, humorous, and intelligent way as a wife, mother, friend, and disciple. The brilliance of this book rests in the fact that Hallie taps into the perennial wisdom of Scripture and her Catholic faith without ever sounding preachy or coming across as better-than-thou. She walks with us on the vulnerable journey that is life, both at its most heart-wrenching and heart-warming moments, encouraging us to stay on the path toward our true home, even if we should happen to fall (a lot) along the way. This incarnational narrative blessed me with a deeper understanding of the mystery that is woman, which is an incredible gift to any man. No doubt it will be a fast favorite of book clubs everywhere, but especially in those circles where women of faith want to cut through the bull and reflect on real life in light of the One who is light itself."

—Fr. Damian Ference, priest of the Diocese of Cleveland and author of *The Strangeness of Truth*

"*Falling Home* is Hallie Lord at her best . . . witty, raw, courageous, and honest. In this little gem, Hallie shares more than words or stories or sage advice; she shares her very heart, inspiring countless souls along the way. Her transparency is refreshing, and this book, vital. I'm excited to share this book far and wide, trusting that lives, marriages, and families will be abundantly and eternally blessed by it. *Falling Home* is a gift to anyone who is tired of trying to hold it all together, and instead wants the peace that only God can give. Hallie is a gift, and I'm proud to call her my friend."

—Mark Hart, CIO and executive vice president of Life Teen International, bestselling author, speaker, and host at SiriusXM Radio

"If you're ready to feel uncomfortable, challenged, motivated, and discouraged all at the same time, read this book! Hallie is honest, raw, and sweet. But I can only recommend reading this book if you're ready to ask questions about yourself and God. Oh, and if you don't already have a therapist, you'll soon be getting one. My own therapist may be buying a third house now that I realize how much more work I have in front of me."

—Lino Rulli, host of *The Catholic Guy Show*, SiriusXM Radio

"In her signature warm and inviting style, Hallie Lord lets us into her longing for a predictable life—and straight into her realization that when the unpredictable happens, the pillars she's built her life upon will still stand. Women who are seeking an anchor in the midst of a storm will find refuge in Hallie's tender guidance."

—Shannon K. Evans, author of *Embracing Weakness*

"Hallie Lord's, *Falling Home* is a resurrection story. A story of a woman emerging from the darkness and seeing with new eyes the beauty of life and the bright love of God. Through her personal, genuine, and raw stories, Hallie reminds us that resurrections are not void of crosses but rather are born of them. She leaves us all with the profound hope that comes from knowing the crosses we carry today are the source of tomorrow's resurrection!"

—Fr. Kyle A. Manno, director of vocations and of campus ministry, Diocese of Rockford

FALLING HOME

CREATING A LIFE THAT CATCHES YOU WHEN YOU FALL

Hallie Lord

An Imprint of Thomas Nelson

Falling Home

Published in Nashville, Tennessee, by Nelson Books, an imprint of Thomas Nelson. Nelson Books and Thomas Nelson are registered trademarks of HarperCollins Christian Publishing, Inc.

The author is represented by Alive Literary Agency, www.aliveliterary.com.

Thomas Nelson titles may be purchased in bulk for educational, business, fundraising, or sales promotional use. For information, please e-mail SpecialMarkets@ThomasNelson.com.

ISBN 978-1-4002-2057-1 (audiobook)

Library of Congress Cataloging-in-Publication Data

Names: Lord, Hallie, author.
Title: Falling home : creating a life that catches you when you fall / Hallie Lord.
Description: Nashville, Tennesse : Thomas Nelson, 2021. | Summary: "Speaker and radio host Hallie Lord shows how to use unexpected hardships and challenges to build a life that will make you more secure and grounded than ever before"--Provided by publisher.
Identifiers: LCCN 2020025728 (print) | LCCN 2020025729 (ebook) | ISBN 9781400220557 (paperback) | ISBN 9781400220564 (epub)
Subjects: LCSH: Consolation. | Suffering--Religious aspects--Christianity. | Failure (Psychology)--Religious aspects--Christianity. | Success--Religious aspects--Christianity.
Classification: LCC BV4909 .L56 2021 (print) | LCC BV4909 (ebook) | DDC 248.4--dc23
LC record available at https://lccn.loc.gov/2020025728
LC ebook record available at https://lccn.loc.gov/2020025729

Printed in the United States of America

21 22 23 24 25 LSC 10 9 8 7 6 5 4 3 2 1

For the one who found the light
in me that I couldn't find.

CONTENTS

FOREWORD

In fourth grade I went on a field trip to the science museum. I and the other students had visited all the exhibits, and we'd even gotten souvenirs. At the geology station, our tour guide had handed each of us a dense, gray rock, about the size of a baseball. It wasn't much to look at, but I clung to this gift. In my child's mind, this was now a prized possession. I thought about how I would display it on my bookshelf next to my badminton participation trophy. It would be a source of pride. When friends came over I would nod casually toward it and mention that I had gotten it when I was hanging out at a museum. And everyone would finally know that I was cool.

Just as we got close to the exit, the tour guide stopped us. He drew us into a workshop alcove where he donned leather gloves and protective glasses. He then picked up a sledgehammer and walked up to me.

"Hand me your rock," he said.

I recoiled.

He was clearly planning to do something with my rock that involved that sledgehammer, and I wanted no part of it. I thought, *I couldn't put a crumbly pile of rock dust next to my trophy! Why would he give us something in the first place if he'd always intended to smash it to bits? Why would he even want to do that?*

"Trust me," he said. He smiled, and some fleeting expression flickered across his face that made me think that maybe there was more to this situation than I realized.

Reluctantly, I handed him my rock.

He placed it on the floor, and I winced as the sledgehammer swung down. With a thud it hit the rock, which broke into two even pieces that shot across the workroom floor. He picked them up, then carefully, as if walking over a birthday cake, presented them to me. The kids behind me gasped. I looked into his hands to see the most beautiful crystals I'd ever seen. Warm pink glittered beneath the purple shards. He moved it back and forth ever so slightly, and the glassy gemstones sparkled as if powered by battery.

I often think God sent me that moment at such a young age because he knew the lesson it contained was one I would have to learn over and over again in life. In fact, even well into adulthood, I still have the same attitude I did when I was a child clinging to that rock. I didn't believe there could be anything better than what I had—perhaps because some part of me didn't think I deserved anything better. I thought I was fragile. I was sure I'd crack and crumble all too easily. So I ran from anything that felt like pressure.

It was in this emotional place that I met Hallie Lord. In fact, one of the things that initially bonded us was a shared but unspoken belief that maybe we weren't strong enough, brave enough, good enough, talented enough . . . simply not enough, period. Yet, as the years went on, something extraordinary happened. The pressures of life grew stronger. The two of us were facing the kind of blows we had always feared, the kind that we had spent the early part of our lives running from. Sure enough, we cracked. We broke. And it was the best thing that ever happened to us.

The Hallie I first met was kind but hesitant, brilliant but consumed with self-doubt. The Hallie I know today, after all those searing trials, is a bold, fearless woman who knows exactly who she is and where she's going. She exudes confidence and energy and joy. She knows that a happy life is something you have to fight for, and she's no longer afraid of those battles, because she is now fully aware of her strength.

These pages serve as a manual for experiencing the same transformation in your own life. Hallie's writing is so vivid and intimate, you'll feel like the two of you are at brunch and she's telling you her stories between sips of coffee (okay, probably a mimosa). You'll get swept away by her inimitable writing style that somehow manages to combine the friendly charm of a chick-lit novel with the mind-blowing insights of a wise monk. You'll have so much fun spending time with her that you won't even realize, when you put the book down, that you have become a different person than when you first began reading.

I still have that rock I got at the museum. It's called a geode. Every time I see it, I think of how tightly I clung to the grey mass it once was because I was afraid that it was as good as it gets. In my timid, fearful mindset, I could never have imagined that the blows of a sledgehammer would reveal such glorious, dazzling colors—that as the hammer swung down, the best was yet to come.

If you need to go through this mindset shift in your own life, you picked up the right book. Let Hallie Lord take you by the hand, bring you into her best and worst moments, and show you the beauty of being broken.

Jennifer Fulwiler
October 22, 2020

INTRODUCTION

CRASH LANDINGS

I know what happens at the end of falling—landing.

—John Green

I have a recurring dream that I am in a crashing plane. We fall from the sky and the plane weaves through trees, barely missing power lines, until it lands with a jarring thud and a loud skid. Sometimes, it careens down a winding road until it runs out of steam and eventually comes to a stop.

The last time I had this dream, the plane crash-landed in the Chihuahuan Desert. Why the Chihuahuan Desert? I have no idea. All I know is that in my dream I climbed out of the plane, chatted with my fellow passengers, and then called family and friends to let them know that I wouldn't be able to make it (to what, I don't know) because, as they may have seen on the news, my plane had crashed. All was well, though, because a group of us passengers were going to hike to a taco stand visible in the distance.

Sadly, there aren't always tacos at the end of my harrowing dreams, but the plane crash does always result in some sort of unexpected benefit. Once, because the crash landing had delayed my arrival to my ultimate destination—because, of course, crash landings disrupt my plans—I had time to stop in a nearby Sephora, the only retail store I have considered moving into. Once I happened to reunite with an old friend while I was waiting for my replacement flight. And, okay, I admit that another time I was mildly annoyed because the plane had crash-landed in a field in the middle of nowhere and all of us aboard had to wait to be rescued by an incoming plane, piloted by an individual who was not overly concerned with the fact that we had almost died. In retrospect, though, I suppose I should have been relieved we weren't stranded on a snowy mountainside having to make difficult decisions about cannibalism.

But in none of the dreams does anyone actually die. Nor is anyone maimed or even mildly hysterical. This is important to note because flying is a phobia of mine, and I tend to lean ever so slightly toward the melodramatic. It wouldn't be out of the norm if these dreams ended with everyone dying harrowing, traumatic deaths. But that's never what happens. Instead, we're all pretty happy—all things considered—in our post–plane crash world. Not because we're not dead, which is a great thing in and of itself, but because we're just happy (or perhaps because of tacos).

In real life, plane crashes don't typically end with happiness or tacos or Sephora. And dreams—though the subject of a long-standing debate—are generally thought to have something to do with our subconscious minds. I'm not shocked that I dream about plane crashes because for a very long time my life felt out of control, and I don't think it's a stretch to connect that feeling with recurring dreams about crashing planes. But the safe landings and the post-crash peace and contentment beckoned me to take a closer look. These dreams seem filled with the kind of wisdom and insight that we say we want but are actually a little scared of, because once we pay attention, we are left with no choice but to do some very painful soul work.

Supposedly, we dream about these things so that all those good and transformative yet challenging revelations we've been running from when awake catch up to us when we are vulnerable and unaware. This doesn't seem fair to me, but God often arranges things in a way that seems unfair to my unripened understanding. (Spoiler alert: In the end, God's way is always annoyingly pretty perfect.)

Lately, I've realized my longtime fear of literal plane crashes represents what I've long feared might happen in my life: a marriage that struggles to be righted, a child who can't be saved, a vision of home that may never come true, and all the little parts of me that might have to crash and burn before they can rise from the ashes and be made new. And in a way, each of these has been the metaphorical plane crash I once feared, spiraling my life out of control as I crouched in the crash position.

Two years ago, I faced the one I feared the most. It was a daunting descent I never saw coming. But as I braced for impact, I realized I was already equipped for the crash. I saw that God had brought me through those prior disasters with fortifications and tools to not only survive but thrive. Those crash landings had made me stronger and more prepared for this current unexpected tailspin. I had overcome my fear of intimacy and had a team of friends ready to build me back up on my worst days. I had healed familial relationships and learned how to keep them thriving even across the many miles that separated us. I had created traditions and habits that helped me put one foot in front of the other even on the most disorienting, painful days. I had devoted time to self-healing and understanding, which helped me navigate my tumultuous feelings safely.

Most importantly, I had entered into a passionate love affair with God. And no matter what life threw at me, I knew his shoulder was and is always waiting for me to rest my head upon it.

My dreams have never been an assurance that, should I one day find myself strapped into a crashing plane, everything will be fine. But they are a reminder that maybe, just maybe, when I feel like life is spiraling out of control and my worst nightmares have become a reality, there might be a metaphorical taco party at the end of it. One that I would have missed out on had God not intervened. Because that's what these crash landings are about, after all. They're about my refusal to listen to the quiet promptings of God when I'm booking my travel through life, leaving him no choice but to send me hurtling toward my divinely ordained destination, whether I like it or not.

This is not to say that when you survive your crash landing—and you will—you won't end up a little battered and bruised. That's inevitable. But rather, you can create a life that will catch you when you fall. You can create a life that is strong and equipped, so that when you go into an unexpected tailspin, you will have ready hands—thriving friendships, healthy family relationships, a solid sense of self, traditions that fortify, and an intimate love affair with God—to guide you to the ground. And post–crash landing, when you stand up and dust yourself off, you will realize you are in a far better place than you would have been had you not walked through fire. Invigorated by the escapade and strengthened by the challenge, you'll have a new confidence and energy in your strut that will make people wonder if Cleopatra and Beyoncé had a love child who happens to be you.

Crash landings, even the metaphorical ones, get a bad rap. Yes, I know, they kind of deserve it. We would all like to be in control, piloting our own planes, planning our own itineraries, and maybe even sipping a little bubbly along the way. But what I am learning, slowly and messily, and often against my will, is that crash landings can shake something loose inside you, something that was stuck, and release you from its bondage. This is what is happening to me right now. A crisis that has turned my life upside down and left me wondering which way is up is forcing me to dig deep and discover my inner warrior—a woman who was always there but had been silenced, hidden by my anxieties, feelings of inadequacy, and unhealthy life circumstances. While excruciatingly painful and often confusing, this process is one of the greatest gifts I have been given. It has given me eyes that gaze up at the sky and, instead of seeing dimly twinkling stars, now see distant balls of fire that are lighting a spark in me.

I want you to find your inner warrior who sees the world through new eyes too. I want you to believe in her when the entire world is telling you she can't be trusted and is not strong or smart enough. I want you to empower her to make all those scary changes in her life that will ultimately free her from bondage. I want you to celebrate her when she ignites the world with her irresistible blaze. I want you to love her.

Because the crashes will come. But if you love her, she will be falling home.

ONE

INTO THE UNKNOWN

Letting there be room for not knowing is the most important thing of all. . . . When there's a big disappointment, we don't know if that's the end of the story. It may be just the beginning of a great adventure.

—Pema Chödrön

I met Dan when I was nineteen years old, right in between the season of life where you try on lots of different identities to see which one fits and where you figure it out. Which is to say that I thought I had a pretty good idea of who I was, but I couldn't have been more wrong. It was not unlike when Charlie, my seven-year-old, slipped his small feet into Dan's shoes, swung a tie around his neck, grabbed his backpack, and declared with pride, "I'm a daddy now!" I had no idea who God intended for me to become, but I had startlingly strong opinions and was pretty sure I could see what my future held.

I love young love. When two people meet each other just as those first rays of adulthood are beginning to peek over the horizon and somehow know that their life together is meant to begin, it can, with a good bit of discernment, lead to some of the richest and most life-giving relationships. Experiencing those early adult growing pains, stumbling and falling, pulling each other back up and out of the dust, and discovering who it is that God is forming within each of you can create wildly strong roots.

But it can also lead to unmitigated disaster if you're not careful. Because, here's the thing: if you try to lay the groundwork for a marriage under the premise that you know exactly who you are and who your partner is, then when you finally do figure it out, you're going to feel a bit wobbly standing on a foundation that was made for another couple.

Imagine plopping a house on a platform made for a houseboat. I have no idea if houseboats have platforms, but bear with me. If you were to do that and then a storm rolled in, all those landlubbing cabinets would fly open and jettison their contents straight onto the floor, where they would lie in a million tiny pieces.

I know this because I am currently standing in the middle of those millions of tiny pieces. What to do with all the pieces is something I am still trying to sort out.

All marriages have good elements and bad, and all go through peaks and valleys. I was prepared for that. I saw it as an adventure that would hopefully lead Dan and me, hand in hand, to heaven. Maybe it will. I know our story is not over. I just don't know the details of how it will look from here on out. I guess nobody ever really does. What I do know is that there is a difference between problems that can unite a couple more closely the more determinedly they work at them, and the cracks in the union that are foundational and get wider and more injurious the more weight they have to bear. I used to think we had the former. For many years I refused to consider the alternative, in spite of all warning signs, because divorce was my *one thing*. The one thing I would never consider. The one thing I would never do.

Then came therapy, that great savior and ruiner of lives. I thought I was just going in for a little tune-up, giving up a bit of my Sephora money to pay someone to listen to me vent for an hour now and then. But I discovered (after it was too late to change my mind) that the moment I sat down on that couch, I had unwittingly signed up to have my life completely and catastrophically upended.

This is why people fear therapy and hesitate to befriend therapists. Therapy is wonderful and healing and true and has a very bad habit of tricking you into doing things you never intended to do. It will save your life, open up worlds within you that you didn't know existed, teach you how to look at things with fresh eyes, and push you to become the bravest and strongest and most honest version of yourself that you can be. But it can be a little sneaky about the whole thing. You have to keep your eye on it or it will try to turn you into a wondrously evolved human being who does hard things in an effort to grow and heal when, if you're being honest, you might prefer to stay a slightly less evolved human being who finds relief in reality TV and mint chocolate chip ice cream. I'm just saying, that's on the table, too, although therapists usually gloss over that part when they're laying out your options.

Now that I think about it, all this growing and evolving is actually my friend Jeremy's fault. A while back he emerged on social media after a long silence and told the world about how he had experienced a profound healing from childhood trauma. He spoke about it like a soldier might speak about war after returning home—bloodied and battered but having emerged victorious. Jeremy exuded relief and was clearly free of a certain heaviness that felt all too familiar. I wanted what he had. I craved it foolishly, like a young adult who is eager to enlist, after having only heard the edited version of war, those stories that highlight the victories and soften the horrors.

Jeremy and I live five minutes away from each other in Charleston, South Carolina. But due to a weird turn of events, we both found ourselves with time to kill in Rockville, Maryland, shortly after his Twitter revelation. We met up for coffee and my interrogation began. Will you tell me more about this healing? How did you find it? Where did you find it? What did it ask of you? Can I have it too? He shared his story with honesty and vulnerability, but I most marveled at how he shared it matter-of-factly. I could sense that his pain no longer agonized him. It no longer played on his emotions without his consent. He was no longer a slave to his wounds and afraid of the shadows that hunted him. Not anymore. Or at least that's what it seemed like to me. I'm sure he would tell a tale of healing that is far more complicated and unfinished. But one thing was clear: he was further along the path than I, and I wanted to catch up.

He passed me the name of his therapist, and I ran into the fire.

Foolishly, stupidly, bravely.

I ran into the fire.

Five years ago I would not have run into the fire. Five years ago I would have listened to Jeremy talk about his deliverance from bondage, looked at my own chains, and decided I actually liked the feeling of the cold, oppressive metal pinching against my skin. It was all I knew, and we tend to cling to the familiar—even if it hurts us—because the alternative is terrifying. Familiar pain can feel weirdly comforting. I would have continued to acquiesce to bondage, because I feared that if I attempted to leap into freedom and missed the mark, I would fall, and nobody would be there to catch me. It was better to remain safe, even if safety meant misery. At least I'd be alive.

We all have areas of life that we refuse to look at, although we suspect that—consciously or unconsciously—they are keeping us enslaved. We tell ourselves stories to justify our blindness, numb ourselves to endure the pain, and paint over the mildew spreading across the walls with fake smiles, instead of breaking them open to find the source of the problem. Deep down inside we know that if we open up those walls, we will discover that the entire building has been built on a faulty foundation, and it will have to be torn down to protect its inhabitants.

I did that for a long time. First with almost every area of my life, then with just a few extra scary parts, and finally with this one last excruciating marital wall.

But as I sat across from Jeremy at the café, I took stock

of my life and decided I was finally ready to march into the one battle I'd refused to engage. I'd been ignoring it and explaining it away for years, but as I watched all the other broken pieces of my life being put back together, I could no longer deny the deleterious effects of ignoring this wall. I knew it would probably be the hardest thing I'd ever done, but I was ready—or at least I thought I was. And if I'm being honest, even after I committed to facing it, I tried to find the easiest path through.

I thought I could control the outcome. I thought I could sit across from my therapist and gather some tools and heal my inner child a bit and be done with it. I even told him about my one thing. I informed my therapist in no uncertain terms that a separation from my husband was not on the table. But the thing about opening yourself up to healing is that you never know what you will find. It's like when you go to the doctor because you've been experiencing headaches or nausea. You know that something is not quite right, but until the doctor examines you and runs some tests, you don't know what exactly is causing your symptoms, or what you need to be healed.

As a small child, I never wanted to reveal wounds or sicknesses to my mom because I was scared of what she might discover. I had lots of phobias about terminal illnesses, and in my immature mind, hiding my illnesses from her meant that I would be safe, while revealing them might cause some dark magic to land me on my deathbed. (As an aside, I told my mom that I have come to believe I don't have much of a problem with depression, but I do struggle a lot with anxiety, to which she replied lovingly, "Yes, Hallie, I know.")

I've always felt compelled to choose blindness over sight. I'd rather stay numb and distracted and in denial than face the truth and deal with it. The moment I sat down across from my therapist for the first time and said, basically, have at me, crack me open, let's see what we find, was probably the single scariest thing I have ever done. But that's what it takes if you really want to get healthy—physically, spiritually, or mentally. It takes opening yourself up and being willing to deal with whatever you find.

You don't have to have a therapist to do this. There is a whole tribe of people online who call themselves "self-healers" with their own method for doing this without professional help. Spiritually wise people can guide you in this work as well. And friends and family, those who love you and know you better than anyone, can be inestimably valuable in your journey. But the first step, the moment of most intense vulnerability, comes when you say, "Okay, it's time. I'm opening myself up and facing the truth, no matter where it takes me." The first step is when you are finally willing to surrender.

My therapist asked me the other day what I wanted. I stared out the window as raindrops fell onto loamy soil and said, "I don't know." It was the most honest thing I knew to say, because I didn't. I'm starting to realize I often don't.

I'm sure there's a category for people like me in the *Diagnostic and Statistical Manual of Mental Disorders*. People who spend more time in other people's heads—wondering what they're thinking, how they feel, and what they want—than in their own. We're working on this, my therapist and I. We're working on getting me all moved out of other people's heads and back into my own. It's a slow process, but we're getting there.

It struck me that, though there's still much work to be done, this place of not knowing isn't such a bad place to be. It's preferable, I think, to the rigid and self-assured land I used to live in.

Being too easily swayed by the opinions of others and not in touch with our own heart and hungers has its own problems. But being immovably sure about things (other than the fact that God loves us incomprehensibly) is a dungeon that puts up a wall between us and Mystery. It essentially tells the Spirit that we have no need for his movements and that we aren't terribly open to illumination. Thank you for the kind offer, it says, but we aren't interested at the moment in being swept off our feet and into a love affair that will take us by surprise and shake us out of complacency.

"I don't know" says, "Humble me, fill me with fire and life, rid me of blindness, free me of spiritual malaise, heal me, make me new, and leave me in awe."

The things we must do to grow—being sensitive to the voice of God, submitting ourselves to healing, and recognizing our weaknesses, motivations, needs, and desires—start with saying, "I don't know." The moment we utter those words, God will take us by the hand and say, "In that case, come with me, my love. What astonishing wonders I have in store for you!"

It took me forty years to get to this "I don't know." It sounds like a lot of years, but in the grand scheme of eternity, I suppose I'm doing all right. And as much as I hate it, and as impatient as I am, I've gained just enough insight over those forty years to know that personal evolution takes time, and God will wait for me until I am ready for him to move in my life.

Many years ago, after having spent the previous night caring for a sick babe, I was taking a nap when one of my sons tiptoed into my room and left a vase of beautiful weeds on my nightstand. I could barely open one eye to behold his gift and utter a grunt of gratitude. But after my nap, when I spotted his gift bathing in the afternoon light on my bedside table, my heart swelled with love, and I was able to respond with fervor.

I think personal growth and God are a little like that. When God eventually gives us the help we have been begging for, the answers we've been seeking, or the consolation we've been yearning for, he wants us to be in a place where we are able to respond with passion and be strengthened and healed by them. He doesn't want us to be too sleepy to savor them. He doesn't want them to fall on rocky earth or thorny ground. He wants to create within us fertile soil, so that all his gifts and truths may take root in us and blossom. He works with us, quietly tilling and turning the soil until it is tender and rich and ready to receive.

That's how it was with me and my marriage. God knew I needed to be healed to do the terrifying work of sorting through what my marriage is and is not. To allow God's healing, I had to be in a place where I could be receptive to his movements. So he kept working on me, coaxing me out of stubbornness and into humility, waiting for me to give up the fight and let him get on with his work.

Some people buckle quickly. They fall on their knees

and surrender to this work God wants to do in them. And they probably do so with gratitude, though it's hard for me to imagine. Other people, like myself, are pretty sure that if God would just hand over the tools and back off a bit, we could handle all the things that need to be handled without any assistance. Thank you very much.

So there God stood, determined to knock down my walls of resistance with crosses of poverty and humiliation, loss and loneliness, desolation and heartbreak, while I, with a stunningly impressive display of fortitude, kept standing back up, chin jutted in defiance, positive that I knew the best way to parent my children, manage my marriage, grow in holiness and virtue, and basically cultivate a life that was pristine and praiseworthy and thriving in every conceivable way.

He must have looked upon me with tenderness, hating to allow all this pain but caring more about healing me and making me whole than saving me from suffering. Each time, whispering in my ear, "Just stay down this time, Hallie. Stay down and let me build you back up." *Stubborn* and *deaf* and *difficult* are all words he could have rightly used to describe me. But instead, he called me beloved. It takes my breath away.

Forty years in, I finally surrendered and stayed down. I finally admitted my powerlessness. I finally invited him in, opened my eyes, and looked around. And what I saw was a marriage in pieces.

I won't lie and pretend that because I stayed down and was finally willing to take a hard look at the realities of my marriage that everything instantly became better. It didn't.

In fact, it got a lot worse. In many ways, it is still terrible and tragic and painful. I don't yet know where this journey will end, and there remains a small fear of the unknown, which is precisely what had tripped me up so often in the past. The unwillingness to say, "I don't know." I don't know what's wrong. I don't know how to fix it. I don't know what the future holds. I don't even know what it should hold or what I want it to hold.

Will Dan and I reconcile? Will we not? Will our relationship always be volatile and complicated and full of pain? Or is there a path to peace wherever we end up? I have to believe in the latter, because with God there is always a path to peace. But I also know that sometimes his peace looks different than what I've hoped for. And sometimes it only reveals itself in the next life. As long as we're talking about peace, I have to make peace with that possibility too.

The path to strength and resurrection and metamorphosis, as contradictory as it may sound, lies in my ability to release my death grip on certainty. I will always love Dan, no matter where our marriage lands. We will always be a family—him, me, and our children. But I am letting go of my one thing. I am letting go of my immovable stance that I will never get divorced. Because as long as I cling to anything stubbornly, I limit God's ability to move me. I want peace and healing and growth for my family, no matter the cost. And I am ready to release myself into the hands of the only one who knows how to lead me to those things.

I am finally willing to let him lead me into the unknown.

TWO

A SOUL SET ON FIRE

Who in the world am I? Ah,
that's the great puzzle.

—Lewis Carroll

I may not always know the specifics of what I want or how best to get from point A to point B, but, after forty years, I finally know who I am. Of course, even as I type those words, a small part of me is wondering, *Will I laugh when I reread this in ten years and think*, Girlfriend, you had absolutely no idea who you were back then? We'll see. But I don't think that will be the case. Certainly, we're all living in a perpetual state of evolution and constantly learning new things about ourselves. But over the past year or two, I've gained peace and confidence in who I am and what God put me on this earth to do. They have settled into my bones. I am no longer so easily hurt by the opinions of others, and I'm far less impressionable than I once was. Now, when I ask myself why I did that thing or reacted that way or made that choice, I am almost always, after a little self-examination and consultation with God, able to answer.

Throughout my mid-to-late teens I was involved in a relationship that was not healthy. And by "not healthy" I mean so incredibly screwed up and absent of any authentic kind of love that it still makes me sad to think about that girl I used to be and the sort of treatment she accepted. And not only accepted but chased after and craved.

When all was said and done, and a few years had passed, my mother asked me, "Why did you stay in that relationship for so long? Why didn't you demand better for yourself? Why did you tolerate such abusive treatment?"

I thought for a moment and answered simply, "Your guess is as good as mine."

Do you know how long it took me to truly understand the reasons? Fifteen years. It took me fifteen years of wondering why before I finally figured it out. And that's with my rounding it down to a nice pretty number.

I stayed because I craved a soft place to land, after having felt for many years like I was being tossed from one place to another without any control over my trajectory.

When I was in elementary school my parents divorced. One day we were all living under the same roof—my dad, my mom, my younger sister, and I—and the next day we were not. The change was extraordinarily difficult for me to process and make peace with. I suppose it doesn't take a genius to know where my one thing came from. If I'm being honest, part of me is still searching for that peace. My parents' divorce came with many logistical difficulties that were hard for me to navigate as a young child, such as remembering to pack everything when traveling between houses and figuring out who to go to with requests for field trip money. Although, to their credit, my parents did everything in their power to minimize these problems, they were still hard to manage. But, by far, the most painful aspect was carrying the burden of their pain. They never asked me to do so, of course. They never even hinted that I should. But I loved them so much that I couldn't help it.

For months, maybe even years, after the divorce, I would wake up in the middle of the night overwhelmed with grief for whichever parent I was not with. I would imagine them all alone in their home, feeling the absence of loved ones. I would cry and cry until my mom or dad would call the other, and they would drive over in the middle of the night to try and reassure me. My parents would tell me over and over again that I could stay at whosever house I wanted and that neither of them would be hurt or offended by my decision. But that seemed impossible to me. I was sure someone was going to end up feeling rejected and unloved and deeply alone.

My desire to create a new unified and stable home was so desperate and all-encompassing that I gave myself over fully to any person who came along and told me I was special or offered to save me.

I wanted nothing more than to take all the wondrous pieces of my childhood my parents had brought to my life—camping under the stars with my dad and making fairy ornaments and delicious desserts at Christmastime with my mom, among a million other things—and toss them into the new home where my husband and children and I lived.

That was my desire, and that was my reason for staying in an abusive relationship for as long as I did. But for years I could not see it. I did not know myself well enough to understand this most obvious of truths about myself and my decisions.

It's interesting to look at my daughters now and see where their strengths lie and where their wounds, insecurities, and insufficiencies will need God to pour his healing. My daughter Zelie, for example, has more self-confidence and self-assuredness than I will likely die with. She was born into the world, all eight plump pounds of her, knowing exactly who she is and the ways in which she plans to leave her mark. It's a delight to see, especially because of how different she is from me. I was born into the world waiting for people to tell me what to believe and show me that I am worthy and valued. Not Zelie. She doesn't need any of that. She needs other things, certainly. We all need something. But she doesn't need confirmation of her inherent dignity and awesomeness. Every confident, happy, and, yes, sometimes cheeky step she takes gives praise to the One who breathed life into her and loved her into being. One of my favorite things about being a mother is learning from my children.

There were other things that took me a long time to figure out, such as: What sort of creative endeavors set my soul on fire? What are my strengths and weaknesses? Which things bring me comfort? Which things cause me anxiety? For years I consistently got inconsistent results on those personality tests that pop up on social media every day, because I literally didn't know which of the offered answers fit me best. That is how poorly I understood myself.

I remember the day I was first introduced to the concepts of introversion and extroversion. A friend had sent me an article about personality types, and it sent me down a rabbit hole and left me sitting on my porch for hours feasting on every last bit of insight Google had to share. Suddenly, so many things I had a habit of doing—things I had long felt ashamed and confused by—made sense. I finally had an explanation, and I felt bathed in giddiness and peace.

For years, there would come a moment, a few days into one of my family's visits to Texas to see our family, when my mom would wander into the guest room at my grandmother's house where we were staying and casually mention that the whole clan was coming over for a big dinner. After hearing this I would always start to cry. Which is insane. And weird. Because I love my Texas relatives so much. Every single one of them. They all have huge hearts and exude warmth and make me laugh. I am always happy to see them and soak them up. But I would literally start to cry and feel awful about it. Not just because I was crying at the thought of having to spend time with people I adore, but because I had no idea why I was crying. That in itself felt unsettling and confusing.

What I learned, sitting on my porch that day, was what 99 percent of the world already knew, I'm sure: my tears were not an indication that I didn't love my family fiercely; they were simply a reaction to my feeling overwhelmed. I am a person who loves people. I love hearing their stories and learning about their lives. I love finding out where they've been, where they are headed, how God has moved in their lives, and what he has taught them in the process. I marvel and delight in the ways people shine and leave their marks on the world. But while some people, mostly extroverts, find such interactions energizing, I find them draining. Which is not a bad thing. It simply means that I need quiet, solitary time to recharge my batteries between times of socialization. When we visited Texas, there would always be a steady stream of visitors, because my grandmother's house was the heart of the family and our primary gathering place. After about three days in, I would crash.

It sounds a little silly, but acquiring this bit of self-understanding changed my life. It brought me peace and made me feel less like a terrible person. It also taught me how to manage my life in a way that allowed me to interact with the world with more eagerness and joy.

A year or so ago, Father Damian Ference was a guest on my SiriusXM radio show, and he spoke about the importance of coming to know oneself. I remember listening to him and feeling troubled that I didn't fully understand who I was. But I knew he was right and that I needed to figure it out. I wanted more epiphanies that mirrored the one I had experienced the day I learned that all my weirdness had a name: introversion.

I also knew that learning who I am at the deepest level was not going to happen by reading self-help books or completing endless quizzes on Facebook. Those things—yes, even the Facebook quizzes—are not entirely without value, to the degree that they lead us to ask important, probing questions about ourselves and to search for answers. But they can never give us the whole picture, because they can never gaze back at us and see who we are and who we were created to become. They can never recognize our uniqueness or see our flaws or affirm our beauty. They can only ever be able to speak at us, rather than engage us, and spit out automated results onto our computer screens.

Only one Person can reveal to us who we are at the core of our being. There are people who may be able to see and reveal to us elements of ourselves. People who can look at our actions and help us search for and discover our motivations. People who recognize our wounds and can show us a path forward to a place of healing. People who can listen to our dreams and wonder with us at their meaning and purpose. But even though their intentions may be good, we all see the world through a prism of our own desires, biases, and life experiences. None of us can know another the way the One who created us out of dust can. So I knew I needed to go to him. And that felt, at first, like a very scary thing.

Scary because God, better than anyone else, not only knows the goodness and beauty in me, but also knows, with perfect intimacy, the areas in which I am sick and broken, angry and hateful, scared and ashamed. I knew that when I approached him and asked him to reveal my innermost being, he would not only say yes but bring every last bit of me to the table and lay it out like a tapestry before me, with all its loose threads and messily woven cords. And I wasn't sure I was ready to see it all. No, actually, I was certain that I wasn't.

I had spent so much time up to this point desperately trying to distract myself from acknowledging all the hurt I had buried deep within. Not because I didn't realize it was there or didn't want God to heal it, but because I was scared of the pain I would experience if I truly looked at my woundedness. I would have to remember the moments that those wounds were inflicted, and then I would have to figure out how to deal with them. Simply contemplating that process felt exhausting.

I would have to journey back to the moment my parents told me they were getting divorced and walk once again through the fallout. I would have to revisit the abusive relationship I had been in and feel again all those feelings of worthlessness. I would have to relive the night he sexually violated me and the next morning when he pretended he didn't know me. I would also have to look at all the awful things I had done to others as a result of my own woundedness: attempting to steal boyfriends because I was so desperate for love; telling lies because I didn't have the courage to tell the truth; and saying the most awful, hateful things to people I cared about because I wanted to clothe myself with the most impenetrable armor I could create, even if it meant hurting others in the process.

I found this contemplation intimidating because I was envisioning myself tackling that big, scary project on my own. I was imagining going through the process of self-discovery and, ultimately, healing, without the consolation of God. But God doesn't abandon us in our pain. And, unlike me, God doesn't withhold mercy when he encounters faults and failures. He gazes at me with eyes of love. He walks right into all my ugliness, sits down, and doesn't make me do anything until I'm ready. And when I am ready, he smiles at me, just as I do with my two-year-old when he has a cut that needs cleaning. God tells me that, though this

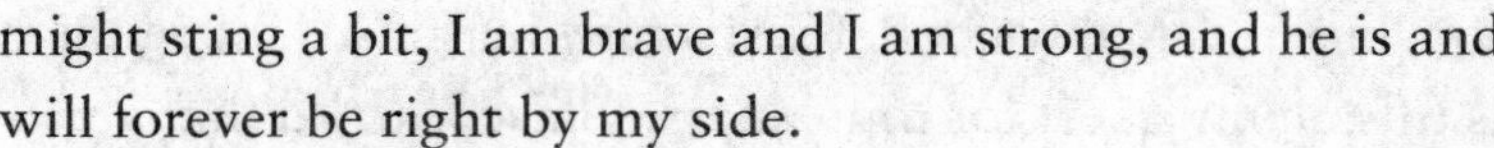

might sting a bit, I am brave and I am strong, and he is and will forever be right by my side.

And so it begins.

He cleans out the dirt and disease and reveals all that is left behind. He shows me who I am underneath the hurt and unveils those intimate parts of me that can only be discovered in an honest and vulnerable encounter with my Maker.

Sometimes God does this in prayer, inspiring us with memories long forgotten and asking us to meditate on them, to enter back into those moments of infliction, and try to make peace with them.

Other times he gently suggests we share our grief with another. In doing so, we bring our fears and pain out into the light so that they may no longer be allowed to hide and fester in the dark, eating away at us. And then, because he is merciful and good, he shows us just who that person is who can help us unpack our baggage, figure out what to do with it, and love us through the process.

Still, at other times, he simply heals us, without our even having to ask, and then takes us by the hand as we look back at where we had once been and who we are now.

We don't come to know and understand ourselves in an instant, of course. The journey of self-discovery is a lifelong process—and even, perhaps, beyond. But God begins his work in us the very moment we make the request, the same moment we assent to his desire to heal us and make us whole. Then it's up to us to receive all that he wants to show and give us. To let go of our penchant for self-deception, to reject pride, and to embrace humility.

And that is good. Painful and hard and intimidating,

too, but undeniably good, for so many reasons. Among them is this: in my quest for rootedness, I have learned that a person can move ten times a year or keep the same address for a decade, but until we rest in who God created us to be, we will always be haunted by restlessness.

So we search and study and beg God to reveal who we are in the depths of our being. And when he does, well, then a new challenge begins. It's one thing to know who we are, but it's another thing entirely to rest in that knowledge.

God gives us many gifts, talents, and personality quirks, and he tucks much beauty into each of our unique souls. Then what do we do? We look over at the person standing next to us and think, *Why am I not good at that thing she excels at? Why doesn't my hair bounce and shine the way hers does? It's not like I don't use Pantene too! And why can't I be as selfless and loving and funny as she is?* In all those questions, we lose sight of what God has done and is doing within us. We lose sight of all the goodness he infused in us. We become consumed with feelings of inadequacy and shame, instead of savoring the gifts God in his inestimable mercy has chosen to give us. And then we fail, lost as we are in our discontent, to use the gifts we have been given to set our little corners of the world on fire. Deep down we know we're supposed to be dancing about, setting these bonfires aflame. But we're not. So we feel restless.

Instead of anchoring ourselves to God and his will with every inhalation and exhalation, we try to break free and pull away so that we can run down other paths that look more alluring. Paths that, through rose-colored glasses, seem to shine more brightly, come with more acclaim, and lead to more satisfaction and higher highs. But these are highs that last but a moment, and satisfactions that will ultimately leave us hungry and yearning. Only once we allow God to reveal his unique plans for our lives and then embrace that vision will we find the peace, pleasure, and contentment we seek.

Being who we are meant to be and doing the work we are given to do means looking around at all the beautiful souls walking the earth, seeing all the fruitful, fertile, impressive work they are doing, and saying, "Thank you, God, for the people who are adding something to our world that no one else could. Thank you, God, for giving them those gifts. Thank you, God, that they have embraced their gifts and are using them. Thank you, God, for giving me other gifts and for allowing me to cooperate with you in other ways. And thank you, God, that when people see me doing the work that is mine and mine alone, I may one day do it in such perfect union with you that through me they will see and feel your love."

That's what I want anyway. That's what I yearn for. Because I can't imagine experiencing a greater level of peace than what I would experience were I to become a perfect conduit of God's love.

A while back I was talking to a friend about a persistent vice I was fighting against. I told him how hard I'd been working to overcome it and how little progress I'd made. He paused, and then said, "What if God hasn't lifted this vice because on the flip side of it lies one of your greatest strengths? What if instead of making it go away entirely, he wants you to ask him to redeem it?"

I told him to stop being so wise and insightful about

everything, because I was far too tired for such an insane level of introspection that particular afternoon.

But his words stuck, as wise words tend to do, and I thought about them a lot over the next couple of months. What if examining my weaknesses was indeed the key to discovering my strengths?

It's the passionate, sensuous people—though they may struggle to temper their hunger for sex or food—who bring the most color into our world. It's the leaders—though they may be bossy and controlling—who bring about profound changes for the better in our world. It's the social butterflies—though they may struggle to sit in silence and hear God—who are there when people need to be seen and heard and affirmed.

My friend was right. God didn't want me to utterly annihilate the aspects of my personality that were less than ideal, such as my predilection for lying in bed for hours binge-watching the *Kardashians* and eating chocolate, instead of doing the laundry. He wanted me to study them with humility and see what they had to teach me about myself. To search for the strengths in them that are hiding underneath, then hand them over to him and allow him to transform them into forces for good.

There is a temptation to fear self-examination and to feel shame when we must confront the less-than-ideal things we discover about ourselves. But the pursuit of self-understanding is one of the most valuable journeys we will ever take.

Life is going to spin you in a million directions and land you in all sorts of unexpected places. In the face of these uncertainties, there are only two things you can know for sure: God will be with you, and you will be with you.

Well, God's ready to go. I'm pretty sure he knows exactly what makes him tick and how to operate at his maximum potential no matter what you throw his way. But you, you are still a wondrous work in progress, and the more self-reflection you do, the better prepared you will be to love, nurture, and guide yourself through anything.

Becoming Cleopatra and Beyoncé's love child isn't easy, but someone's got to do it.

THREE

WILDNESS AND WONDER

What is home? My favorite definition is "a safe place," a place where one is free from attack, a place where one experiences secure relationships and affirmation. It's a place where people share and understand each other. Its relationships are nurturing. The people in it do not need to be perfect; instead, they need to be honest, loving, supportive, recognizing a common humanity that makes all of us vulnerable.

—Gladys M. Hunt

Even though I grew up in California, I've always held a little extra love for Texas in my heart. I believe that Tex-Mex is an official conduit of God's healing power, that inner tubing down a lazy river is just about the greatest thing anyone could ever do on a Saturday afternoon, that there's nothing in the world quite like when a bolt of lightning cracks open the big Texas sky and sheets of rain pour down, that Blue Bell ice cream has no rival, and that bluebonnets are some of the most beautiful flowers in existence.

When Dan and I got married and started our life together in Alabama, I always took for granted that eventually we would move to Texas. There we would buy a house covered in stone on a quiet residential street with a giant oak tree in the backyard to which we would tie a tire swing. I thought four children sounded like the perfect number—two girls and two boys—and I would don beautiful aprons in our sunny kitchen and bake more pies than my family knew what to do with. I pictured our kids riding their bikes to the public school down the street every morning, and I would meet them on the corner every afternoon. We would spend as much time sitting in our porch swing as we did on our living room couch. I figured Dan would work a typical nine-to-five and I would be a stay-at-home mom; that is, until the kids were older, and I would find a part-time job. Then Dan and I would skip from continent to continent after retirement.

Basically, I envisioned the life my maternal grandparents had led. Our traditions, day-to-day routines, and long-term goals would look just like theirs. I didn't realize it at the time—it wasn't a stated goal—but this was the dream that the young-adult me quietly held in her heart.

We did move to Texas about five years into our married life, and we did live in a house covered in stone. But beyond that, reality looked nothing like my dreams. The joy and peace I expected would be present simply were not. We didn't do the things I thought we would do, and I didn't feel the way I thought I would feel. Dan and I struggled and fought and grew further and further apart until we became two people I didn't recognize. I couldn't understand why this was happening in Texas, the place I'd naively assumed would be our utopia, the place I'd hoped would save us.

I fought hard to make it work, but in what was one of the more painful decisions I have ever had to make, we chose to pack up and head back to Alabama.

For a long time, the story I told myself, the story that seemed to be true, was that Texas just wasn't a good fit for Dan. He didn't love it the way I did. It hadn't sunk into him as it had into me. But the truth, which I discovered much later, was that Texas was simply not the place God had chosen for our family to settle at that point in time. Texas culture was not the culture that this new family Dan and I were building together was meant to adopt and make our own. Bluebonnets would not be our official family flower.

Things got a little better during our second stint in Alabama. We stayed for a while and found comfort in the familiarity of it—and also the ocean, which is where my heart feels most at home—but still we struggled. There seemed to be great chasms between Dan and me that we could not fill or cross. We would speak and speak to, and sometimes scream at, each other, but neither of us seemed able to hear or understand. We loved each other but often did not like each other much.

And then we moved to Ohio.

Ohio was not a place I had ever dreamed or imagined we would make our home, even temporarily. I barely knew where to find it on a map. But a promising job presented itself, and in that season of life, promising jobs were enough to make us do crazy things, like packing up five kids and moving to an area of the country about which we knew nothing. Ohio, as it turned out, was not a great fit for us either, but I will forever be grateful to it, as it gave us one of the greatest gifts we have ever been given: our family.

We were a family already, of course: me, Dan, Daniel, Jack, Sophia, Lucy, and Zelie. But until Ohio, it was as if Dan and I had each been holding on to either end of a bungee cord, neither of us willing or wanting to disconnect from each other yet determined to walk in opposite directions, creating tension. In Ohio, we turned and sprung back toward each other, and this time we stuck.

We stuck, because for the first time we were in a place with no family and very few friends. We had set off, just the two of us and our little tribe of merry babies, on this adventure. Isolated from the influence of others and forced to find our own way, we were able to finally see the unique vision that God had for our family. We found our family culture. We found the things that animate our singular little tribe. Even if one day should Dan and I no longer be united in marriage, those things will remain true.

It took a while to get to the point where I could look around the dining room table and see this new and unrepeatable thing God had made for what it was, because for a long time I possessed two problematic personality traits: I was impressionable, and I was afraid of hurting people's feelings. Being open to other people's opinions and availing yourself of their wisdom are not bad things. But when you take that receptivity and twist it a bit, you find yourself blindly following anyone who has given you the slightest reason to trust or admire them—sometimes into utter disaster. Being empathetic is a beautiful thing too. And a heart shuttered against the suffering of others is a dead thing. But I let my empathy for others, especially those I loved, turn into a fear of ever doing anything that might cause them pain, and the fruits of that were not good.

Parents might be called over and over again to make decisions that may not be to the liking of your loved ones. Those loved ones may express displeasure at your decisions, and that can be a difficult thing to endure, loving them as you do. But when you are desperately trying to create a new family, with its own unique identity, being far too easily led and even more terrified of inflicting hurt upon them is poison. Or maybe it's more like a virus. The sickness didn't just damage me; it tried to weaken and destroy everything Dan and I were building.

In Alabama there was his family, and in Texas there was mine. When we got to Ohio, we discovered that what we desperately needed was room for our family to grow and breathe and stand on its own. We needed to try on different traditions for size—some his, some mine, some entirely new to us—to see which fit our family best. We needed to set our daily life to a new rhythm, one that could only be tapped into by listening to the song God was singing to us. And we needed to see one another through lenses not obscured by the identities our extended family members cast upon us.

Ohio gave us those things.

We didn't stay long—just nine short months. And of all the states we've lived in, Ohio is the only one that did not see me give birth to a baby. But I now think of it as the place where our family was born. We set off for Charleston, South Carolina, as a new family. A family that was established, healed, and strengthened. A family that was eager to discover what God would have us do and become.

Courage is contagious. It is a virtue I very much want my children to possess when they one day leave home. I pray that they never lack the bravery and daringness required to surrender to God's curious movements and follow him wherever he may lead them. And I hope the fact that Dan and I don't seem to be able to resist doing weird, crazy, unusual things for the same reason will aid them in this endeavor. Because one day God will knock on their doors and say, "Boy howdy, do I have an adventure for you!" And after hearing God's insane plan, I hope they will pause for a moment and think, *Well, this isn't any crazier than what my parents did that one time, so, why not?*

Establishing your family culture, discovering what God would have you do and become, requires courage. Because there is a lot of pressure out there, both societal and familial, to keep up with the Joneses, to make sure you're checking off all the boxes that a "normal" family should be checking off. There's pressure to let your kids do what all their friends are doing, and to honor your family's heritage because Aunt Nellie will be very upset if she comes to your house for Thanksgiving dinner and beholds a buffet that contains different food from the variety she was served as a child. And also, if you could not be "too weird" about everything, that would be great.

We are failing at this last part in a super big way.

But I am okay with being a little different because I don't

really have a choice in the matter, and it sends a message to my children that it's okay to be the unique, wonderful creatures God meant for them to be.

It's okay to be a little odd. It's okay to view the world a little differently than your friends. It's okay to be quiet or loud or both. It's okay if your talents and interests are kind of unusual. It's okay to have different priorities from the rest of the world. And it's okay to go against the grain or the tide or whatever your family and friends and neighbors and that stranger at the grocery store think you ought to be doing.

It's better than okay. In fact, it should be cultivated and celebrated.

Dan and I had lots of babies because we love babies, and we sometimes let those babies sleep in our bed because they are yummy. We are not what the world would consider financially responsible, because we like the aforementioned babies more than reliable bank accounts. For the most part, we don't do team sports or a ton of extracurricular activities, but we create art constantly—music and books and paintings and sketches—and we play that music and read those books to one another and tape that art up all over the walls. We prioritize our faith above all else. And we love dessert. And dance parties. And lazy Sunday afternoons spent in our pajamas.

This is who we are.

Do we do everything perfectly? Nope. Do I worry that I am ruining my children because I can't give them everything they want? Because I possess a higher number of deficiencies than average? Because sometimes I look at our life and think, *We really are crazy, aren't we*? Yes.

But at the end of the day, do I rest in the knowledge that God knew what he was doing when he made me their mother and Dan their father? That he knew what we would and would not be able to give them? And that all those things—both the gifts and the absence of gifts—would be exactly what they need to become the magnificent creatures they are meant to become and live the lives they are called to live?

I really do.

When I was pregnant with my first child, I closed my eyes and tried to imagine what this new little life growing inside me might look like. I pictured Dan and I walking through our neighborhood in Midtown Mobile, Alabama, pushing a stroller holding a plump baby girl with raven-colored hair, an Amélie-esque haircut, big blue eyes, pink cheeks, and alabaster skin. I can still see that baby vividly when I close my eyes.

That baby looks nothing like any of my babies. Also, my first child ended up being a boy. That was just a baby that a new eager mother dreamed up while she waited impatiently to meet her real one.

We do that a lot as parents and husbands and wives. We dream about what our lives and children and relationships might look like. And most of the time it's just that. Harmless dreaming with no threat of disappointment attached.

But sometimes we do become attached to those dreams. We imagine that our children will share our love of sports or that our spouses will delight in spending hours roaming flea markets for that perfect corner table missing from our living room. We imagine that our spouses will handle and approach things in the same way our beloved parents did. We imagine that our families will go on camping trips every summer or to the symphony on weekends or read aloud together around the fire every winter night or collect a great many domesticated animals and maybe occasionally an odd undomesticated creature or two. Sometimes we don't even realize we have been dreaming these dreams until we discover, with surprise, that they don't fit into the actual family and lives God has given us. That they don't fit the people we love.

That can be a painful realization. Why wouldn't all the lovely, happy things from our childhoods be in our adult lives? Why wouldn't our children delight in the same things we did? Why wouldn't our spouses see how the traditions we grew up with could perfectly carry over into our new families?

Because God is creating a new thing. And we need to leave room for him to work.

This is not to say we shouldn't mourn the loss of things we thought might be or fight for the elements of our hopes and dreams that are most important to us. Rather, my point is that when we overwhelm our lives with unchecked expectations, we choke out all the actual goodness God wants to pour into our families.

I have a friend whose husband was captain of his varsity high school football team for three years. From a very young age his every waking thought was of football, and probably his dreams too. He had inherited this love from his father who inherited it from his father, and every Sunday they would all gather for games in matching leather chairs.

So it made sense that my friend's husband assumed that his first child would carry on the tradition. But then his son was born, and from the moment he could hold a pencil, his every thought was of art and storytelling and imaginary worlds. This led to years of grief as my friend's husband had to wrestle with the death of a dream he had held for years. There were few things he wanted more than to spend Sundays watching games with his son, and later watching his son play in those games. He loved his son dearly, but he didn't understand him, and for many years he struggled to bond with him.

Then, on the day of his son's high school graduation, that same father watched with tears in his eyes and a grin on his face as it was announced that his son had received a full scholarship to the California Institute of the Arts, arguably one of the best art schools in the country.

My friend's husband turned to the stranger on his left and said, "That's my son!" with all the pride in the world. Then he turned to his wife and said, "I just want him to be happy. That's all I want." He had finally made peace with their differences, and from that day forward, his relationship with his son flourished.

If we imagine that our ideal child will possess certain characteristics and passions and preferences and discover that they don't possess any of them, we blind ourselves to the actual beauty that God has tucked within them, unable to see what God is so eager for us to discover and delight in. If we project an image onto our spouses of what a perfect partner looks like and they come up short, we deny them the opportunity to shine in the singular way that God created them to shine. If we envision that a good life must adhere to certain narrow and specific parameters, we miss out on all the wildness and wonder that is waiting for us.

Here is what we can expect from God: He will tell beautiful stories with our lives and take us on spectacular adventures. He will heal and transform us, and we will be astonished by our transformations. He will give our families unrepeatable, distinctive, and perfect identities because they were crafted for us and us alone. He will, through these things, overwhelm us with peace and a sense of rootedness. And he will never, not even for a moment, stop loving us.

We can expect these things.

But he doesn't promise that it is always going to be easy. Or that he will protect us from pain. Or that he will not ask us to bend and change and adapt. Or that our lives will look as we expected them to. Honestly, life never does. Why? Because we don't dream big enough dreams or desire with big enough passion or yearn with big enough longing.

But God does.

His dreams will astound us because he can see things we cannot. His desires will satisfy us into the depths of our beings because he knows better than we do the nature and root of our hungers. And he yearns to give us all these things simply because he loves us.

So what happens when we say goodbye to our unrealistic expectations and open wide our arms and surrender and accept his gifts and love unreservedly?

Well, that is how a family is made.

FOUR

MORE THAN IT IS

People who love to eat are always the best people.

—Julia Child

It wasn't the clear lancet windows or the milk-white steeple or the stately walls of salmon-colored brick that stirred my heart. It was the way in which these things captured my imagination and reminded me of what was hiding inside. The nave with its shy, sweet tones of swan's eggs and the elegant brass chandeliers. The crisp prayer books and the quiet, concealed corners that have beheld the depths of grief and the heights of ecstasy and everything in between. I have only stood within and outside the walls of St. Francis Episcopal Church in Potomac, Maryland, a handful of times, but still, in its own small way, it feels like one of my homes away from home. The sight and thought of it calls to mind funerals and weddings and Sunday services attended with my Maryland-dwelling dad's side of the family. Driving past it even for a moment causes my heart to surge with love and makes me feel instantly and intimately connected to them.

Other places scattered across the country invoke similar responses in me. Austin, Texas, for example, where I was born, lived for four years, and have been visiting ever since, holds many memories. Every time I drive through the winding roads of West Lake Hills, where my uncle lives and my grandparents once did, I think about all our Ramsdell family gatherings. The Barton Springs Pool, with its thousand feet of natural limestone, reminds me of hot summer days spent swimming with family in the perfectly ice-cold, spring-fed water. The Hamilton Pool Preserve, when I call it to mind, immediately takes me back to moments of racing down the trails, leaping over exposed roots along the path, eager to find the waterfall at the end. And the Guadalupe River. There is no other place in the world that can make me hunger for the hot, black inner tubes and soaking-wet Keds and the smell of sunscreen the way it can.

Northern California, too, where I spent almost sixteen years of my childhood, has countless of these places. The Redwood forest in which I spent endless hours hiking with family and friends. The Point Reyes with its lighthouse, Mendocino with its artists, and Santa Cruz with its campus slugs and boardwalk. The breathtakingly tempestuous Pacific Ocean with its anemone-rich tide pools and the dramatic cliffs and funny blowholes that surround it. Just thinking about them, even from almost three thousand miles away, makes me feel united to my family.

We have lived in Charleston, South Carolina, for over five years now. I would love it if God means for us to stay here. We shall see. But already, in so many ways, it feels like home. I know its roads, and I'm beginning to understand and love its natives. The weather, with its mild winters and hot, sunny summers complete with afternoon rainstorms, feels as if it were made for me by God himself. The historic district's cobblestone streets, horse-drawn carriages, and pastel antebellum houses will likely never stop delighting me. And the beach on Sullivan's Island, which can be reached only by traipsing through dunes covered in wild natural grasses, soothes my soul in a way that few other places can.

But while filled with memories that capture and remind me of times spent with my husband and children and friends, Charleston is almost entirely absent of memories that include my extended family—cousins, aunts and uncles, grandparents and parents, and my sister. I don't walk down its streets and remember our times of laughter and sorrow and connection.

I don't feel them here with me in this place.

When I talk to friends who have also moved away from the place they once considered their home about the challenges of being uprooted, they all say the same thing: it's not the new place that causes them pain but the absence of the old. They grieve the loss of familiarity and the daily reminders of treasured memories. It's the severing, or what feels like a severing, of their ties to a place that knit them together with those they love most in the world.

It's okay to grieve and be a little sad, or sometimes a lot sad, that we can't pick up and pack up and take our favorite swimming holes and theaters and restaurants with us. It's hard to leave those things behind and start a new life. To put new seeds in the ground and watch them grow. To create new memories. And it's okay to acknowledge that.

But I didn't want that to be the end of it. I didn't want it to stop with sadness and acceptance and move on. I wanted to find a way to bring my memories, the ones that in an instant could make my heart swell with affection for those I miss, into the new places God was leading me.

In the end, the answer came through my favorite things in the entire world: snacks and a small child.

It was August, or maybe September, and hot beyond what I felt was a reasonable level of hotness, which was something I was silently telling God as Lucy and I pushed a shopping cart through the aisles of our grocery store in search of snacks. Snacks, because we were going to the swimming pool, and you can't go to the swimming pool with a passel of young ones without snacks in hand. Snacks, because they are delicious and good.

We paused in the chip aisle, where Lucy grabbed two bags of FRITOS and then looked up at me with her giant brown eyes, seeking permission to deposit them in our cart.

"Perfect, Lucy! And make sure you grab the bean dip too."

"What's bean dip?"

And that's when I realized that I had utterly failed this child in every conceivable way. But not before being swept into a visceral memory of things I had lost since moving away from Texas. FRITOS and bean dip and warm, sunbaked peanut butter and jelly sandwiches. Ice-cold drinks dripping with condensation. And Big Hunk honey-sweetened nougat bars with peanuts woven in. All of them being consumed on the banks of the Guadalupe River with my family, whom I missed so much.

Rope swings attached to thick tree branches. Swinging them over the river and letting go. Plummeting into water and bobbing back up full of laughter. Wet bathing suits and dirty tennis shoes and warm skin and sandy towels. The smell of the hot earth. Skipping rocks and spinning on inner tubes. Laughter. So much laughter.

One beautiful memory after another filled me up with joy.

"Bean dip, Lucy," I said. "I can't believe you don't know about the bean dip."

And then I told her. So that even though she had yet to experience them all for herself—the river and the snacks and the love—she would know her people have a story, and she is a part of that story.

While I may not be able to carry places with me, I could bring food to any home.

Like the cheese toast my grandfather, my Opa, would make me every morning of our summer visits. Just as the sun was beginning to peek out over the horizon, he'd grab a piece of bread, spread it with butter, top it off with slices of sharp cheddar, melt it under the broiler until bubbly, and cut it into tiny bite-size pieces (crust cut off, of course). He always served it with a side of tiny breakfast sausage smokies. Then he would blow on them softly to cool them off, so I wouldn't burn my tongue. He loved me tenderly, and the cheese toasts made sure I'd never forget.

And the ambrosia that only my mom and I would ever eat, though we would eat enough for the whole family. Now on Thanksgiving and Christmas, even though we're states apart, we never fail to call each other to make sure we have added enough sour cream to the bowl full of mandarin oranges, pineapple tidbits, chopped pecans, shredded coconut, and marshmallows. Because to eat ambrosia that is not adequately juicy would be a terrible tragedy.

And the cheesy potatoes made by my dad. I have yet to master them—to make the potatoes soft enough, brown the onions just right, or melt the cheese so that it is soft and gooey on top and crunchy on the bottom—but I have not given up trying. And each time I do, I think of him.

And the fudgesicles in the freezer, Juicy Juice in the refrigerator, and meat loaf at night at my granny's house in Maryland. Having been raised a vegetarian for the first few years of my life, meat loaf was not a dish I would have expected to enjoy. But when she made it, I was surprised that I did.

And few things make me feel as loved as chicken pot pie. Every time we would travel to Texas, my grandma Virginia, my Nama, would serve it for dinner on the first night, simply because she knew how much I loved it. She was also a wonderful teacher. She was so patient in the kitchen that my pot pie tastes just like hers, which instantly transports me back to her dining room table with all the love and laughter that surrounded it.

So much has been written and said about the power and beauty of breaking bread with one another, and indeed it is a powerful and beautiful thing. But I am finding that breaking bread while apart, when united by a common memory, can also bond people together, reminding them of what's important. It makes the distance—even if that distance spans one life and the next—feel a little less vast. That's how much grace God has poured into bread, into food. That is how much he loves us.

In fact, he loves us so much that he gave us food to begin with. He didn't have to do that. He could have easily come up with some other way to nourish us. Some way that didn't involve our getting to experience the bliss of a juicy peach exploding in our mouths on a hot day, buttery mashed potatoes drenched in gravy, crispy bacon, warm tomatoes with milky mozzarella and bright-green basil, creamy chicken tikka masala on a bed of rice, heavenly Tex-Mex, or pie à la mode with coffee. He didn't have to give us any of these gifts. He didn't have to create those funny little things known as taste buds. But he did, simply because he loves us, and it delights his heart to see his children experiencing pleasure.

This blows my mind.

It's not just the familiar food itself that lowers the drawbridge of separation and sends those feelings of connectedness to far-away family. It's the act of eating, too, like the unique way in which our family of ten approaches feasting. It is chaotic and crazy and wonderful and so closely resembles every meal I can remember sharing with my beloved Texas family.

When my children were little I went through a phase where I devoured books about homemaking. I learned how to make a sink shine and a quarter bounce on tightly tucked sheets and how to make floors so smooth that my kids could skate across them in their socks. I learned how to soak dirty clothes and defeat stains and make laundry smell absolutely delicious. I learned about daily and weekly and seasonal cleaning routines. I even made a homemaking journal to organize all these tips and tricks and schedules. And I learned about setting a table and making it warm and welcoming. (Honestly, the whole thing was a little out of control. It only stuck for about three months and twelve days.)

But what these books didn't teach me was how to keep all the little bottoms that I consider mine firmly planted in their chairs. Perhaps I needed a parenting book for that. Or a book about overcoming your genetic makeup, because eating with bottoms planted firmly in chairs isn't traditionally how the Ramsdells (my mom's side of the family) approach the consumption of food. And I very much feel like a Ramsdell when it comes to such things.

No, the Ramsdell clan approaches each and every opportunity to eat as if it were the greatest social event in the history of the world. We chatter as we round the buffet filling our plates. We chatter as we settle into chairs and couches or sprawl across the floor. We chatter as we return to the kitchen for seconds and maybe thirds. And we chatter as we dig into our desserts, sometimes three to a plate. We chatter and laugh and tease each other mercilessly all the way through.

I had forgotten how much I loved this approach to breaking bread when I first became a mother. I imagined a calmer and quieter, more tranquil and serene, daily dining experience, at least at dinnertime. This wasn't a rejection of family tradition. I just didn't think it through. Also, I get funny ideas sometimes.

I saw dripping candles that somehow didn't tempt little hands. Beautiful tablecloths that didn't end up irredeemably stained after first use. China that didn't get chipped. Glasses that didn't fall over and nearly tumble to the ground. Bodies that were calm and didn't wiggle and loved sitting still. I also heard soothing music playing in the background and soft, quiet voices. (That last one makes me laugh the most.)

This was a beautiful vision, and I wanted and expected my children to be able to fit into such a scene should they be invited. But it wasn't God's vision for our family life. At least not on a daily basis. What God saw and desired well before he tucked the first babe within my body was children leaping up from their seats with big, bright eyes and expressive hands waving in the air, so excited to share the incredible ideas that popped into their heads. He saw babies on laps and food on the floor and an endless supply of sippy cups. He saw hysterical laughter and voices talking over one another and occasional arguments, and a mom trying to restore maybe just a bit of order but secretly loving all the craziness. He saw singing and stories and joy. So much joy.

That's what God saw, and that is what he created, and that is what we have come to embrace.

Is it messy and chaotic and not fit to be documented within the pages of *Southern Living*? Well, yes. But that's what life is when lived to its fullest. It's also where we will find God, and where he finds us. It's where he feeds, nourishes, and comforts us. And it's how he brings us together.

Every time we break bread together, we are remembering Christ's gift of self, the single greatest act of love ever carried out. That is what breaking bread is all about: love. And love isn't always, or even usually, subdued or restrained or picture perfect. It's wild and messy and often doesn't look like how we had envisioned it. But regardless of how unique our family cultures, day-to-day routines, and mealtimes may look, they all have that one thing in common, because they are emulations of God's love for us as manifested in holy communion. They become one of the primary places where we are seen, known, and loved.

When we come together to have dinner, we are given the opportunity to notice one another. Who is unusually quiet? Who seems sad? Who is bouncing up and down, eager to share something? Who is especially happy? We see each other. Then we can ask about the quietness, the sadness, the eagerness, and the happiness. We can listen to the answers and come to better know one another. And ultimately, we are given the honor of loving one another as we soothe and comfort and guide and celebrate together—as we break bread and share in God's inestimable, untamed, intimate love.

This may be my favorite part of family life. Especially now, during this time of upheaval, instability, and change in my life. Gathering around a table with my small and no-longer-quite-so-small kids, checking in with them, asking them about their favorite part of their day, and consuming food together brings me a visceral sense of comfort and familiarity. I need that more than ever now.

Don't let perfection be the enemy of the good. Gather when you can. Let the cups spill and the china break. Eat the frozen pizza and the ice cream sandwiches. And laugh at the diva-ishness of the toddler screaming at you.

Don't stop gathering. Don't stop communing. Don't stop finding and loving one another amid the madness and messiness of life.

FIVE

SUNDAES ON SUNDAY

This is what rituals are for. We do spiritual ceremonies as human beings in order to create a safe resting place for our most complicated feelings of joy or trauma, so that we don't have to haul those feelings around with us forever, weighing us down. We all need such places of ritual safekeeping.

—Elizabeth Gilbert

My Nama died recently. I'd visited her just months before, when I was in Austin for a business trip. Somehow I knew it would be the last time I saw her, even though her death did not appear to be imminent. I sat next to her and soaked her up. I thought about how sitting next to her felt like sitting next to a big bunch of freshly cooked cinnamon rolls. Warmth and a sweetness surrounded her. She made you feel love.

On the way to the airport, my aunt Genie, who inherited

Nama's sweetness, mentioned, independent of my own conclusions, that she thought this might be the last time I saw my grandmother. We sat with that knowledge for a moment, not ready to let her go but happy in a bittersweet way that she might soon be free from Parkinson's disease, which had been causing her increasing suffering and frustration.

When I got the call that Nama had passed, I was sad, of course, in that slightly muted way before the loss really hits you. But I also remember thinking, *She has so deeply sunk into me. She is so much a part of who I am and how I see the world that I don't think I will ever feel completely separated from her.* And I don't. I see her in my movements and decisions and perceptions, in the way I stroke my children's hair and kiss them goodnight, and even in the way I apply my face cream at night—which is, naturally, of the same brand and variety that she used. Though she and I stand on either side of the thin veil between this life and the next, I feel her love intensely.

I picked out a few things of hers to take with me when I was in Texas for the funeral: her KitchenAid mixer, a set of pearls that my grandfather had given her decades earlier with the yellowed receipt still tucked inside the box, a collection of slightly used lipsticks from Clinique (always Clinique), and her well-worn, much-loved Bible. Though I only had a moment to wander through her home and select a few items to remember her by, each one that I chose felt perfect, as if I were guided by God, and her, in the choosing.

The KitchenAid mixer reminds me of the hours we spent cooking together and of the recipes that she would cut out and send to me with a few words of wisdom scribbled in the margins. I can still see her winsome handwriting clearly in my mind.

The pearls remind me of her marriage to Opa. She was his "Valley View," so nicknamed because he thought she was as beautiful as the view gained from standing atop a mountain and gazing at a magnificent valley. They loved each other with the kind of passion that only reveals itself when, underneath it, there exists a steadiness born of years of trial and triumph. I love romantic love so much because she loved it first.

The lipsticks from Clinique, such gorgeous, brightly hued lipsticks. At her memorial service, we watched a slideshow of her life set to music, and several times it was pointed out that she was never without her lipstick. For her, it wasn't about vanity or some misguided sense of propriety but about the joy that those splashes of color brought. This is true for me, too, and I now wear one of her lipsticks almost every day. On the days that I don't, they are still with me, tucked into my purse. It brings me such pleasure to know that the same pigment that touched her lips now touches mine. That in this way, we are similar and united.

The item I most treasure among all is her Bible. When I grabbed it from her shelf and asked whether I might inherit it, I imagined the joy and peace it would bring me to hold in my hands the same manifestation of God's Word that she had held in hers. To see the delicate, worn pages and know that they had become so because she had handled and flipped them back and forth and soaked up their essence many times. What I hadn't known, hadn't even thought to expect or hope for, was that on several pages she had added thoughts and meditations in her beautiful script. And on more pages, she had underlined words and phrases and passages that had resonated and stuck out to her. To be separated by life and death and yet still be able to experience the miracle of God together is a mystery I will never fully understand but will forever cherish.

All these things my grandmother gifted to me are reminders that she gave me a deeper sense of rootedness. This is something I am learning, something that I must be ever cultivating if I seek to create a life that will catch me when I fall.

When I was in elementary school, I built a simple tree house in the evergreen that stood outside my bedroom window. Day after day I hoisted two-by-fours up into the tree using a rudimentary pulley I'd designed and tied them together with rope until I had a little platform to sit on. Then I constructed a roof out of colorful umbrellas so that I could sit in my tree house as the rain fell around me.

I've always wanted a home of my own. From as far back as I can remember, I dreamed of finding a little piece of land with a humble house set on top of it. I wanted to go out into the backyard with the seeds that would become my life in hand, dig a hole in the land that was mine, and send roots down deep into the earth.

I wanted warmth, love, traditions. I wanted loud moments and quiet ones. I wanted holidays that filled the house to bursting with grandparents and parents, children, aunts and uncles, and cousins. I wanted to know my neighbors so well that in the morning I could fetch the newspaper in my pajamas, robe, and slippers. And I wanted to bring those same neighbors bubbling casseroles when death or new life visited their homes.

I wanted a porch swing that squeaked because it had soared past the living room window so many times. I wanted a home my kids could return to from college and be able to lay down their burdens in the same room where I'd rocked them to sleep as infants. I wanted a place with scribbles on the walls from measuring my children as they grew toward the sky, a tree house in the backyard inhabited first by my children and then later their own children, and a kitchen that had collected the scents of an infinite number of family dinners. I wanted this all.

Again, I wanted, though I couldn't have articulated this at the time, to re-create the life my grandparents had created. Only later would I realize that what I really wanted was not the details of their life but the stability and the constancy I found in their home. No matter what life threw at me, or how topsy-turvy it got, their home represented a safe haven. And I desperately wanted a safe haven.

As it turned out, God, too, wanted me to have a safe haven. He simply had ideas about this sort of thing that rarely lined up with my own.

In the years following my wedding to Dan, I clung to my narrow vision of rootedness. While learning to mother, amid diapers and lullabies and mountainous piles of laundry, I daydreamed endlessly about what our forever home might look like. I bought piles of home decorating magazines every month—*Southern Living* and *Domino* and *House Beautiful*—and nearly made realtor.com my home page and repeatedly reminded my skeptical husband that if we don't play the lottery we can't win (or, in our case, put down a deposit on a home).

But then God showed up and knocked on Dan's door and told my husband—who had previously been doing things like touring the country, writing music for Warner Bros., and talking to bigwig music managers in Los Angeles about representation—that he thought it might be a good time (the perfect time, come to think of it) to put the band to bed and start a new adventure, like going to graduate school, getting a degree in theology, and eventually, working for the church. A job whose profit sharing would prove to be more heavenly in nature than earthly and require us to move around a bit, that is, twelve times in sixteen years.

I would love to be able to say that I handled this interruption to my plans of staying in one place with grace, having so clearly seen God's hands in the steering. The truth, though, is that for a long time my longing for a home, for roots that dove down deep and dug deeper, kept me from fully engaging in this life. This longing was a source of great pain. But, as he is known to do, God showed up, with all of his little merciful lessons surfing right within the waves of my grief.

He said, "Don't you know, my little vine, that plants can survive relocation? Moving from place to place is no threat to their ability to thrive. What they cannot survive is a lack of nourishment. I will give you a home, but it will be one born of strong, healthy roots so that you may stretch heavenward, growing ever closer to me, rather than one that is deep and immovable."

"Well," I told him, "I'm open to a touch of personal growth. But if you wouldn't mind, I'd really rather do it in a stable environment with a very low risk ratio and no huge surprises."

Then he laughed at me, in that loving, patient way of his. Because what he knew, and what I am still learning day by day, painful lesson by painful lesson, is that soul-level growth most often happens when God and life and terrible things push me out of my comfort zone, and I yield. When I long for one thing but love demands another, and I acquiesce. When I stop fighting and surrender.

My grandmother taught me that rootedness, at least as it relates to family, doesn't always mean we get to live side by side. But that, by virtue of our closeness, our roots are intertwined; they drink and eat from the same soil. We walk through life encountering and experiencing things together, even when we're separated by many miles. We take in those things, fall in love with some of them, learn about ourselves from them, and allow them to feed and shape us in some way. Because we do much of them in union, there will always be an overlap of varying degrees between the things that make us who we are and the things that make our loved ones who they are. And from these overlapping elements, we discover—no matter where life may take us, geographically speaking—a sense of belonging. For me, as someone who has moved often while craving stability, this revelation has been a source of comfort.

My grandmother walked in the love of Christ, and for a long time, because of my bias, prejudice, woundedness, and agnosticism, I didn't imagine that to be a path we would ever walk together. In fact, when I first met Dan, one of my friends asked me teasingly whether there was anything

I didn't like about him. I paused, then in all seriousness replied, "Well, I think he might be a Christian, but I'm sure we can work through that somehow." I wasn't wrong as it turned out. But little did I know how that would work out.

Though my grandmother was quiet about her faith, it was always there, whispering to me through the steady stream of peace that accompanied her through all of life's highs and lows. I always knew she possessed something I longed for. I just didn't know what it was.

Saint Francis is often credited with having said, though he likely did not, "Preach the gospel. If necessary, use words." That is exactly what my grandmother did. She was deeply private about her faith, but her life was a walking gospel. She was clothed in humility and selflessness and exuded charity and kindness. She made her entire life a gift of sacrifice to those she loved. She tossed seeds of love into the air, and they fell onto the ground and took root in our family. I wanted to be just like her. And later in my life, when I started to search for God, I knew I had found him when I discovered a faith whose Spirit felt just like sitting in the presence of my grandmother. She and the Spirit felt so intimately like home to me when I so wanted and craved a home. So home I came.

Much of the hunger for rootedness that I carried with me throughout my life was satisfied simply by discovering where I was headed. I now know that my ultimate destination, my final home, is heaven. There is something so comforting in knowing that I am journeying toward a place I long for, even if I am not yet there. Hopeful anticipation is not a bad state of mind to be in, and I find it vastly preferable to yearning for a sense of rootedness that seems ever elusive. But God is not content to simply quench our thirst. He wants to pour his mercy down our parched throats and make us drunk on his love and goodness. He wants to inebriate us. He wanted to inebriate me.

Often, when we ask God to fulfill the desires of our hearts, we limit him to a narrow vision of how we want those hungers to be sated. I sometimes wonder whether my hunger for home could have been satisfied sooner and more fully had I better appreciated the unique and mystical ways God fulfills our desires. I wanted a house on a small plot of land in a community where we would live our entire lives. I wanted my desire for a sense of home to be met in that very specific way. But God isn't limited by our lack of creativity or our stubbornness. He can walk right into our desires and fulfill them in a million different wonderful and perfectly unique ways. While I had been trying to turn God into a magic genie, he had been working to make my heart whole. And succeeding. It just took me a while to recognize it.

For a long time, when I envisioned creating family traditions, I imagined taking my kids to the same Memorial Day parade every year, discovering our secret and ideal spot from which to watch the fireworks on the Fourth of July, and seeing the same Christmas tree lighting every November in the same town square. Those are not things you can do when you move around a lot. You can go to parades and watch fireworks and see tree lightings pretty much wherever you are, but they won't be your parades or your fireworks or your trees. And that made me sad.

God sees all these community-centered traditions and delights in them endlessly, I'm sure. But he also has infinite ways he can fulfill the longings of our hearts, regardless of our personal circumstances. So he peeked into my heart, saw that what I wished for was good, and offered me another path. One that was even richer and more soul stirring. One that could be packed up in boxes and carried around the country. And one that was inextricably linked to me.

He offered me seasons of fasting and feasting, times of penance and celebration, Advent calendars and Christmas trees and Easter baskets. White first holy Communion dresses and the cutest little man tuxedos. Days to celebrate the saints and pray for the poor souls. Candles and cakes and soups on Fridays. Ice cream sundaes devoured over laughter in our kitchen after church on Sundays. And then he sent me a whole passel of tiny ones whose eagerness and hunger for tradition exceeds even my own.

At the last baby shower I attended, we went around the room and offered advice to the new mom. When it was my turn, I said, "Don't start any family tradition when you have one child that is not scalable to the realities of life as a family of ten." I was half joking. But knowing that my friend also dreamed of having a larger-than-average-sized family, I was somewhat serious too. I had longed for family traditions that were unchanging from year to year, and so my children took that as a challenge and answered, and continue to answer, with a level of zeal and intensity that is equal parts exhausting and everything I ever wanted.

Should I ever forget to order our Advent wreath from our favorite tree farm in Maine, there will be a revolution in my home fit to rival the zeal of those young French men who scaled the barricades. My children are merciful and loving and good, but they aren't playing games when it comes to their liturgical year celebrations. So far I haven't forgotten the wreath, but I did neglect to create our toothpick-pierced salt dough crown of thorns this past Lent, and my children are still looking at me with bewilderment and concern.

I also set our wreath on fire one Christmas Eve. Or maybe Dan did. It's hard to say. My memory of the incident is murky up until the point that our fire alarm went off. We rushed out of our bedroom, where we were slaving away for Santa, and saw flames reaching up from our dining room table to kiss the ceiling.

I lost our baby Jesus (and then found him). I had to rush out late at night because the Easter Bunny forgot all about the new baby at our house. I tried to begin a tradition of celebrating my children's baptismal anniversaries about twenty times. I'm still trying because the pope thinks I should, but the pope should also know that if I reach my twenty-fifth attempt and fail again, he's going to need to pray for me an extra lot.

But even in failures, traditions are created. Dan and I now joke about calling down the fire of the Holy Spirit on our Advent wreath, and the kids have asked numerous times whether the baby Jesus will be joining us on Christmas Eve or perhaps later in the season once Mommy manages to rescue him from wherever she tucked him away for safekeeping.

There is a rhythm to our years, as seasons come and go, and no matter how often we have to pack up our bags and boxes and move to a new address, these things come with us. They not only come with us but also aid us in making the hard transitions.

The first thing we always do after we turn the key and

step into a new home is haul in our box of crucifixes (yes, there are so many they need their own box) and hang one in every room. Then we bless each room with holy water and say a prayer of thanksgiving and petition. Thanksgiving to God for giving us a place of shelter in which our family will continue to grow and change, and petitions for continued protection and guidance.

To an outsider it might look a little crazy watching all ten of us march from room to room, spin in circles until we found the perfect spot for Jesus to reside, sprinkle water on the walls, and talk to God. But beyond the deeper meaning and the grace contained, having these be the first things we do in any house gives us a sense of peace and grounds us. It is our way of saying to God, "We have checked in to this new adventure. We may still be feeling a little apprehensive and wobbly, missing and mourning the things we've left behind, wondering what the future holds, but we trust in your love for us, and we give this house that you have given us back to you. Please make it a home full of warmth and happiness and security." I mean, it's a lot more chaotic and disorganized than I just made it sound, but the essence is always there, comforting and uniting us.

Of course, once that is finished, the unpacking begins, and the thing about packing and unpacking the beloved treasures of eight children is that something always gets misplaced. Every single time. There is no way around this. No Pinterest or HGTV-inspired solution is to be found. It just is what it is. But treasured items bring comfort and security during big life changes. So back to our ancient traditions we march, seeking aid.

Saint Anthony is our go-to guy for locating missing items. He is, after all, the patron saint of such things. "Saint Anthony, Saint Anthony, please come around. Something's lost and can't be found." That's one of the first prayers my kids learn because something is always lost in our house, and their mother has been known to show a startling lack of interest in such crises.

A while back, Dan was putting together gym equipment in our garage and a tiny (truly minuscule in size) screw was lost in the process. All nine of us searched and searched and searched for this screw. I was not terribly surprised at our lack of success because our garage contains piles and piles of those things that a large family collects and needs but definitely doesn't want inside the home. But Dan was determined. He suggested we pray to Saint Anthony for the swift recovery of said screw. We prayed, and when the prayer concluded I went into the house to check on dinner while everyone else resumed searching. When I walked back into the garage not five minutes later, someone had found the screw. That's how awesome Saint Anthony is.

All of these traditions—the ones born of living life together and the ones that emerge from breathing with the church—offer us an abiding steadiness and a sense of peace that is immune to disruption. Our new houses and neighborhoods and towns may feel a little unfamiliar and ill-fitting at first, but we always feel at home because we are rooted in something that transcends our earthly circumstances. We are rooted in the supernatural, which is at once divine and everywhere and earthly and anchored in the dailiness of our lives.

I am rooted in prayers to Saint Anthony and sundaes on Sundays. In elaborately decorated birthday breakfast tables and nightly blessings bestowed on my children's foreheads. In chicken pot pies that smell like my grandmother's home and the yellow quilt that looks like it. In feasting and fasting. In the popcorn and cranberry strands that hang from the branches of our Christmas trees.

I am rooted in these things even as everything around me is changing and demanding that I evolve. These are things I cling to and the places where I find my stability, even on dark days when the path before me seems to have gone missing. These are, in fact, the things that have given me the courage to change my life for the better. When I feel intimidated walking down previously untraveled roads, I know I can take these rituals with me and rest in their familiarity.

I may not be steeped in a history of unchanging experiences born of a permanent address or a particularly stable life. But I am rooted nonetheless in all the traditions, big and small, temporal and spiritual, that have sprung forth from love and were created and given to me by Love itself.

SIX

CLEMENTINE

The darker the night, the brighter the stars, / The deeper the grief, the closer is God!

—Fyodor Dostoyevsky

I have strangely strong convictions about Christmas trees. It is my belief that real, sap-bearing, intoxicatingly good-smelling Christmas trees are the only acceptable kind of Christmas tree. I've heard that in the case of severe allergies, dispensations may be available, but you'll have to talk to God about that. He's much more understanding and less rigid about these things, I suspect, than I am.

I am, I'm relieved to say, slightly more reasonable about the sourcing of said trees. Tree lots with real trees that spring up on the roadside just days before Thanksgiving are fine with me. Lovely even. Especially if they have signage telling me where their trees were born and raised. I like to know a little about my trees prepurchase, so that I can love them better and more fully.

But if you really want to do it right, you'll have to drive to a Christmas tree farm, borrow an ax, march into the woods, and cut that tree down with your bare hands. This is something our family does approximately every four years when the moon, stars, and planets all align . . . and our children happen to be in seasons of reliably decent to good behavior.

So it was in 2016. We all piled into our unusually large and cumbersome van and headed west out of Charleston to the nearest Christmas tree farm. Per our tradition, it was Gaudete Sunday, the Advent season's Sunday of joy. The perfect day, we've determined, to go tree hunting. We listened to Christmas carols on the radio while clutching festive drinks in our hands. A small babe, just eleven weeks along and the size of a fig, was tucked inside of me, newly discovered and deeply loved.

At the farm the kids cooed over the piglets and dashed between the haphazardly planted trees. Soft rain fell and dotted their eyelashes. Dan found a tree for us and strapped it to the top of the car while I tried to keep track of the one-year-old.

It's a funny thing to look back on those moments of pure, innocent joy, knowing, only in retrospect, that sadness and grief were already on their way.

Moments after we walked back into our house, I began to bleed. It was, as any woman who has ever had a miscarriage will understand, the kind of bleeding that leaves no doubt. Our baby, our tiny Clementine—so named because all of us had a strong sense that I was carrying a girl, and because I couldn't stop chugging orange juice—was leaving my body, had left this earth, and was already tucked within God's arms. I like to imagine my sweet babe like that, tucked into the crook of God's arm.

As the sun set and midnight grew nearer, I began to hemorrhage. When I fell to the bathroom floor and vomited while my ears rang and the room spun, unable to even prop myself up on my elbows, Dan carried me to the car and drove me to the hospital.

Nobody likes to sit in an ER waiting room, but still, it's a little disconcerting when the hospital staff take you straight back into the bowels of the facility without even stopping to ask for identification or insurance information. I fought to keep my eyes open as sleepiness settled over me like a heavy blanket. The nurses asked me over and over again to tell them my name and date of birth, even though my husband stood by my side and was, I thought quietly, perfectly capable of answering such silly questions. I thought that if they would just let me be for a few moments, I could get the most delicious sleep. I wanted to sink right down into the pillowiness of the bed, stay there for a while, and be at peace.

They knew this, of course, and knew the dangers of this pillowy sleep I craved. So they kept asking me my name. I considered offering a different name just to keep things exciting, but suspected that were I to do so, they would double down on their efforts to keep me away from the enticing sinking I was determined to make.

I thought then of the exhaustion I experienced in the last hours before I gave birth to my first child, Daniel. The sensations were similar, but only one was rewarded with a slippery, fat baby while the other brought only emptiness and longing. *Better to sink*, I thought.

But God disagreed.

A friend once told me I should write down the times God showed up and loudly announced his presence when I needed him most, so that I would remember how much he loves me on the days when he seems too busy to lend a hand. He's never too busy, of course, and I know this. But from time to time he's very, very quiet while he does his work in me, which I sometimes find a little annoying.

He wasn't quiet when we lost Clementine.

No, when we lost Clementine, God showed up and threw a huge farewell party for the girl whom he had, in his infinite wisdom, decided to take home far sooner than we would have chosen. There were tears, as there usually are at farewell parties, and deep grief over our loss. But there was also an overwhelming and surprising joy. In fact, there was so much joy that, instead of naming her Clementine Penelope as we had planned, we named her Clementine Joy, our girl who could spin beauty out of bereavement.

God brought presents to the party too. Only these presents weren't for our daughter, who was now in a place where every desire of her tiny heart was already being fulfilled, but for her mom. God knew I desperately needed some gifts I previously hadn't been willing to open. They were gifts of love and gifts of grace and gifts in the form of lessons to be learned. They all came with the same card that simply said: "Let us love you, sweet girl."

My experience of this not-aloneness began with my

husband, who held me as I bled and listened as I said over and over again through tears, "I'm so sorry," fearing that I had caused this somehow, either by a failure of self-care or dearth of love. It was a ridiculous fear to have, but when it is your body that bears the marks of a life lost, it doesn't feel ridiculous at all. It feels like you once had the honor of holding the most precious gift in the world and, though you didn't mean to, you dropped it.

Dan held me close, tilted my chin up with his hand so that I could look him in the eyes, and said, "Don't ever say that again. Don't you ever think that. It's not true." And he kept saying it until I believed it. This was the first of many whispers from God that I leaned on, and I would be held up by a tribe of people who cared for me—some of whom I didn't even know—as I mourned and questioned and healed.

Little signs that God was near were all around me. Our priest, Father Mark, arrived with holy oil and anointed my hands and forehead as he prayed over me. A nurse lovingly told me she understood the magnitude of our loss. And when I was taken into surgery, the nurse who was removing my jewelry unclasped my Miraculous Medal, which bears the image of the Madonna, and said gently, "I have to take this off, but don't worry, Mama Mary will stay by your side the entire time." Kindnesses unasked for, mercies freely given.

When we were expecting our first child, I told Dan that I didn't want to share our happy news with anyone other than family until the first trimester had passed. The thought that I might miscarry and then would have to share the pain with others horrified me, the deeply private person that I was. But my sweet husband just couldn't contain his joy, and days later he admitted that he had been unable to keep the news a secret when he bumped into an old friend at work.

This is the right approach to new life. Celebrate it and make a cake and share that cake and top it with ice cream and let all the people who love you wade with you into the highs and lows, the euphoria and bliss, as well as the fear and mess and uncertainty. We were made for one another, all of us strange people wandering the world together. Made for communion. Made to share joy. Made to be foolish and vulnerable and honest. Made to be one another's solace in storms and lights at the end of, and even within, the tunnels.

It took me a long time to learn this. It took the loss of my daughter for me to learn this.

It was never the sharing of joy that caused me to hesitate to announce a new pregnancy; it was the potential sharing of grief. I've never been good at letting people sit with me in my pain. Pain is a vulnerable place to be. Some people are good at keeping on their armor, only sharing what they feel moved to share while suffering. I am not. When the waves of grief or shame or hurt crash over me, they take my armor with them and leave me exposed, unable to hide my mess.

So there I stand, surrounded by my mess. The crumpled, tear-stained journal entries that tell stories of heartbreak. Old bandages that have covered stubborn, festering wounds because I refused to take my God-given medicine. The threadbare, dirty blanket I would hide under when I felt embarrassed or ashamed. Discarded boxes of food and empty shopping bags, the evidence of all those times I tried to anesthetize myself with temporal things. And the broken glass from the time I threw that cup against the wall.

It's ugly and shameful, and it's hard for me to trust others in that space. What if they want to box up the mess and throw it out before I'm ready to let it go? What if they're disgusted by it and by me? What if they spin slowly in a circle, looking at it all, and feel pity for me? What if—and this often feels like the worst outcome of all—my pain causes them pain?

Here's the thing, though, about having had seven healthy, uncomplicated pregnancies. You start to feel safe. Bulletproof. You conclude, not with any sense of superiority but just as an assumed statement of fact, that you are not a woman who has miscarriages. You are aware that there will be pain in motherhood but think that it comes later, after the bliss of birth. So, with this false sense of security, you let down your guard. And being so overwhelmed with love for the new soul nestled inside you, just like your husband, you begin to tell everyone you meet.

In my case, this included not only my loved ones but also the listeners of my SiriusXM radio show and, as my grandmother once affectionately referred to them, my little internet friends. Now I had to tell them all that my tiny Clementine was gone. That I feared I'd dropped her. I had to let them sit in that with me and allow them to see my mess.

It is difficult to feel at home in this world when you refuse to let your fellow inhabitants become your family. When you walk around holding everyone at arm's length, you end up feeling a little like a stranger in a strange land (though, hopefully, with far fewer martians around), perpetually existing with your guard up, loving only a small number and fearing a great many, and rarely fitting in. I will probably never be a person who has a bursting inner circle. The friends I love deeply (and mildly obsessively) can be counted on one hand. And this is okay. This is, I believe, how God made me. But when God crafted my unique mold, I don't think he intended for me to hold myself at such a distance from others. I know he didn't. I just didn't know this before we lost our little Clem.

The next day, back at home and tucked in bed, ears still ringing, I took to social media and shared our news, fearful that if I didn't, people would see the pregnancy announcement I'd posted recently and continue offering their congratulations. If I could have stood the thought of that, I would have waited a long time, gathering courage in small spoonfuls, before speaking of her death.

But I did share, and the most extraordinary thing happened. Thousands of people rushed in with bucketfuls of love and drenched me. Some brought meals while others sent messages, expressing their sympathy and, with a level of vulnerability I hadn't previously been able to muster, sharing their own stories of loss. Friends showed up and whisked our kids away so I could rest, and I don't know that I've ever had so many people praying for me. I received flowers and found gifts on our front porch.

I felt deeply loved.

Even more amazing to me, though, was that no one commented on my mess or tried to fix me. Everyone just sat with me, as if all the refuse that I hadn't yet found the time or inclination or courage to get rid of was the most normal thing in the world. It was, and we all have it. I think that when we look at the "mess" of someone else's life, we see a great story being written, with a brave and resilient hero at the heart of it. It's a lot harder to see when we're standing in the middle of our own wreckage, and why I believe it's so critical that we learn to be vulnerable and lay ourselves bare in front of people God puts in our path. Standing a bit outside of the mess, they can change the narrative for us and reveal to us what God sees when he looks at our lives: beautiful transformations in progress.

We buried our girl at a cemetery near the sea, its trees dripping with Spanish moss. When we arrived on that startlingly cold day, we discovered the plot that had been chosen for us in the baby garden was directly next to the resting place of a dear friend's little one. I thought in that moment that maybe God was showing off a little, and my heart swelled with such love for him.

As I stood at Clementine's grave, I was consumed with the thought, *This place, both physically and spiritually, where I love and miss and mourn and long for a person I never got to meet—this is where I am meant to find God. This is where he heals me.*

God has a million ways to heal a soul, and over the course of our lifetimes, he will likely employ them all, caring for us so fiercely as he does and wanting so desperately to fill our wounds with his love. I knew in that moment that he was going to take all the pieces of my broken heart and put them back together in such a way that it would feel less like a heart that had been mended and more like a heart made new.

On the way home, we stopped by our PO Box to pick up our mail. I turned the copper key in the lock, pulled open the door, and gazed in wonder at a mailbox so stuffed full of Christmas cards that I had to bend, manipulate, and pull forcefully to retrieve them. And then, just as they were set loose in my hand, a key fell onto the floor.

I picked it up and walked around the corner, searching for the number engraved on it. Moments later, I opened a second PO Box and discovered that it, too, was full of Christmas cards. Unable to carry all the cards in my arms, I had to borrow a plastic mail bin from the woman at the counter and take them to our car. After returning the bin, I climbed into the passenger seat and stared speechless at the pile of cards in silent wonder. My kids bounced from their seats and grabbed with delight at the red and green and silver and gold envelopes.

After I shared the news of my miscarriage online, people from all over the country, simply out of the kindness of their hearts, asked what they could do to support us while we grieved. After giving some thought, I replied that, if they happened to be sending out Christmas cards, we would love to receive one. I have a long-standing love affair with snail mail. It is a source of daily joy, by which I mean I love my mailman with a deep and abiding affection that probably makes him feel a little uncomfortable. When I thought about what small thing might lift my spirits, the idea of getting to see all those smiling faces imprinted on Christmas cards and sharing in their cheerfulness made me happier than almost anything else I could think of.

But I never could have imagined that so many people, most of whom I'd never met, would take time out of their busy lives to send us a card. As I opened those cards one by one and read the messages of love and condolence, something inside me broke open.

For the first time, I understood that all those feelings I'd carried around of not being rooted to any one community or tribe were of my own making. For so long I'd held everyone at a distance for fear of letting them into my pain, and as a result, I'd refused to allow God to love me through them. This joy, this new and intense closeness I felt to God, even amid all the pain and grief I was experiencing, was the fruit of my finally opening the door and welcoming people into my life. Of all the graces God had given me after losing Clementine, learning that he desired to care for me through others and that, if I would just allow him to do so, he would pour into my life more love than I could fathom was the choicest.

If you want to live a life of daring, a life that rejects complacency and yearns for transformation, a life that asks more of you than you have to give, you need others. I think this is why I remained stuck for so many years. The loss of Clementine proved to me the truth of what I had known but failed to grasp: I can do hard things, brutally, painfully hard things, but not without the support of others.

A year later, we found ourselves once again happily dragging a Christmas tree into the house on another unusually cold Advent day. And once again my body held a little one inside of it. Only this time, she had reached full plumpness and was ready to be born at any moment.

I took a nap upstairs while Dan and the kids trimmed the tree. I thought about how a year ago at this very moment I had discovered that our Clementine Joy was gone. I meditated on how much had changed since then, and on how grateful I was that God had met me in my pain and healed so many parts of me that needed healing.

When I stood up to go back downstairs, I heard a small pop as my water broke, and God handed me my last gift. A few hours later, in the same hospital where I'd said goodbye to our daughter, a little girl gazed blinkingly up at me and took her first breath in my arms.

We named her Penelope, a name gifted to her by her sister who overwhelmed us with her joy.

SEVEN

FOR ALL ITS TEMPORARINESS

Beautiful places are not just a joy for the moment, while you're there. They will become homes for you, spaces of solace and comfort, where you can close your eyes and go to. Nothing you experience will ever go away. It belongs to you now. Just feel. Don't be afraid to feel.

—Charlotte Eriksson

When I met my friend Sarah, she lived in a beautiful home that looked like it should be featured in *Better Homes and Gardens*. The bones of the house were lovely. It was clear that the architect who had envisioned it loved the work. What made it extraordinary, though, was that if I had wandered into the home without knowing whose it was, I would have been able to instantly tell that it was Sarah's. It had her fingerprints all over it, from the wall of family photos to the cozy reading nook to the buffet in the corner that alternated between being a hot cocoa station, a waffle bar, a wine bar, and an ice cream sundae stand. Every corner spoke of her love and devotion to her family and friends.

But life happens, and sometimes things go south for a while before they head north again. After digging deep, Sarah found herself standing in a marriage that had to end. God was leading her out of one kind of life and into another. In the process, she had to say goodbye to that home in which she had nursed babies and broken fevers and spun love and fought with everything she had to save her family. The home that had been the beneficiary of countless hours of her attention and passion as she sought to create a haven of peace and encouragement. The home that held a literal record of her family's growth, both spiritually and physically, on its walls. She had to say goodbye to it all.

She had a lot of things to mourn during that time, but the one thing I expected would knock her to the ground with grief was the loss of that house. My image of her taking down the curtains she had sewn with her own hands and boxing up many more precious memories felt like it would be too much for her to bear (and they weren't even my curtains or my memories). But when I showed up at her house to help her pack, she met me with a smile. Granted, it was a smile that held heartache, but she had not broken into two, and there was hope etched into the laugh lines that stretched out from her eyes like the Low Country rivulets that appear and disappear with the changing tides.

She was still smiling.

I gently asked her, as we dismantled one season of life and packed up its pieces to bring to another season, how she felt about moving. It was one of those questions that you immediately regret asking as soon as it leaves your brain and takes up audible space in the universe. *How could she possibly feel anything but bereft and heartbroken and fearful?* I thought. Clearly I still had much to learn about the resilience of the human spirit and sustenance of God. She smiled at me—a real, joyful, if not a bit conflicted, smile—and said that she couldn't wait to throw paint on this new blank canvas of a home God had given her.

That level of optimism and surrender leaves me deeply concerned about the state of my own soul.

Sometimes when I look back on my adult years and at the many little assumptions I have made about myself and my motivations, I am deeply relieved that there is such enormous value in the journey. I am thankful that it's not all about reaching the destination because, boy, I have gotten it wrong so many times and have taken an unprecedented number of detours. But that's okay, because we try things on and cast them off when we find that they don't fit quite right. And through that process, we move a little closer to the truth of who we are and why we do the things we do, and who God wants us to become. If we can put the fear aside, that's a fascinating adventure to be on.

Because we've moved, my family and I, twelve times in sixteen years, I've always hesitated to put much time, energy, or money into decorating any of the beautiful homes God has given us. I told myself that it was a waste of resources, knowing that in all likelihood we would have to pack up and start over in a new home anyway. That the pieces I had so lovingly chosen for one home wouldn't fit right in another.

But as I stood in Sarah's kitchen, watching her wrap up the plates on which her family had broken bread together, I realized I'd been telling myself a lie the entire time.

It wasn't the resources I was trying to protect. It was my heart.

To invest in a place is to let it have a little piece of your soul. It's saying, "Here, I give this to you. This meal with all of its delicious scents that have soaked into the walls, this scribble in the corner that can't be completely wiped away, these words carved into the tree in the backyard. They are all yours now, to remain forever in this place." When you have to walk away from that place—as we have had to do so many times—and leave those things behind, there is grief. Though I didn't realize it at the time, and can only see it now in retrospect, I was determined to minimize that sense of loss and pain. So I would place the furniture and perhaps hang a picture or two, but I wouldn't imbue our home with all the singular and wondrous things that gave it our family's essence. I wouldn't let it have more of me than it absolutely demanded.

Of course, I am not as much the master of my domain as I'd like to think. I am surrounded by small people with big ideas, and because I love them and want to make them happy, in many ways they lead the charge when it comes to how we live our life. As they have grown older, they have taken an interest in transforming our houses into homes. As children often do, they grabbed my reticent arm and yanked me where they would have me go, which in this case was on a mission to make our dwelling places reflections of our innermost beings.

Our most recent home, an actual literal dream of a home—that is, if you're using *literal* in a nonliteral way—was given to us by God. All good things come from God, of course, but when this good thing came along, God made himself so visible that he might as well have walked up to our front door, knocked twice, and handed us the keys.

It all started on Easter Sunday when I piled our small tribe of fantastic creatures into our car and went for a drive so that Dan could hide the eggs without distraction or obstruction. The kids and I go on drives together not infrequently, as I have found this to be the only legal way to restrain them when they are in desperate need of restraining. So we know the roads and streets and avenues of our small South Carolina town well. We know the traffic patterns of the busy roads and the best route to the treasured and lovely secret spots. We have a path that goes by Starbucks, one that leads straight into the Chick-fil-A drive-through, and another that passes both for the days when we're all in need of blessing and rescue from certain death.

We know our town.

In this town there is one street, a drive actually, that is better than all the rest. The lots are large and private, the trees are beautiful and dense, it ends in a cul-de-sac, and there is even a river that runs lazily around and beside it. People don't get to live on this street unless they have lived there for a very, very long time, because no one in their right mind would ever leave. And judging by the fact that I've never once seen a For Sale or a For Rent sign on all my drives, that is not far from the truth. At least once a week I would steer us down this street and daydream about how one day God might lay a miracle right in our lap and allow us, too, to live on this magical street. I'd never told God that. But he knew, of course, because he knows everything that goes through my mind and that I hold in my heart. He likes it, though, when I tell him. When I visit with him throughout the day and give him little updates about things.

So on this Easter Sunday, I told him about my dream of being counted among the lucky ones who got to live on that particular street. It was a silly little prayer that went something like this: "Hey, God, so I know you know this already, but gosh, I sure do love this spot. I know I'm dreaming the impossible dream, but oh my goodness, would I love to live here one day. Crazy, I know, but there you go." Then I left it alone and forgot all about it.

Seven weeks later, on Pentecost Sunday, it was Dan's turn to buckle up most of the kids and take them out for a drive. They were headed to church, while I stayed home with the ones who were sick and couldn't go. But they were early, and so they decided to meander through the surrounding neighborhoods. About fifteen minutes after they had left, my phone rang. It was Dan asking me to write down a phone number. He said he had just driven by a house with a For Rent sign in the front yard. Our current home didn't have a backyard, so we had been dreaming together about getting one on a large lot. He didn't have time to stop by but wanted to call later to inquire about the property. Then he asked me to write down the address. He was probably a little concerned upon hearing me cough, sputter, and nearly choke on the water I was drinking.

The house was on my street. The one I'd fallen in love

with. The one I'd just told God all about but, for some inexplicable reason, had yet to tell my husband.

Detachment is not a thing I'm great at. When a possible fulfillment of a dream flies about me I run after it, trying to catch it and make it mine like a crazy woman, butterfly net in hand. This time, though, I couldn't bear imagining what could be because the whole thing just seemed too insane. And, most likely, too expensive. Dan, on the other hand, thought he should pop over and take a look at the place. Just to see.

I stayed home.

When he came back, he reported that the house was everything we had ever wanted in a home. Not only that, it had not been rented yet and the landlord seemed eager for our oddly large family to reside in it, which was a miracle in and of itself. The monthly rent was a bit higher than we might have hoped, but that wasn't the biggest hurdle to overcome. The biggest hurdle was that we would have to come up with a not negligible sum of money to cover the deposit as well as the first and last month's rent. And quickly.

This prerequisite was somewhat painful given the unlikelihood of our being able to pull it off. But it also came with a good bit of peace, because I knew either God was going to show up in a big way or he was not. Either way, his will would be made pretty clear. This is not to say that I was completely chill about everything—God heard a whole lot from me over the next couple of days—but I was comforted by the memories of the utter disasters that had befallen me when I had tried to force my will on a situation. Those are strange things to be comforted by, but if you had seen the disasters I'd created, you would understand.

So we crunched some numbers, prayed for a miracle, and asked our closest friends to pray for us, too, all the while remaining vague about the details. And then we waited.

The next night I received a call from my friend Ally. She is sweet and humble and doesn't ever want to step on toes. If she tells you God told her to do something that in any way involves another person, rest assured, God told her to do it.

She said she almost didn't call because she was so worried about offending. But her husband, Burt, told her that if God had moved her to this action, then all she had to worry about was following his directives. Which is such a beautiful and simple yet powerful way to approach life. Poor God. I bet he wished many times that I would adopt this approach, instead of having to hear me constantly say, "Are you sure, God? To be honest, I'm not so sure you've made the right call here. Let's examine it from a few more angles . . ."

Unlike me, Ally did listen to God. She didn't argue with him. She called me as she was moved to do, and what she told me blew my mind. She said God had told her to pay the deposit and the first and last month's rent for this home we were praying about. She had no idea this was exactly what we needed. None. But God knew. So he turned to her, knowing that she is brave and selfless, kind and generous, and asked her to be his hands and feet. She was and continues to be that for us and others. I love her dearly.

One month later, on what was to have been our tiny Clementine's due date, we moved in.

I could almost see God standing on our porch and

opening the front door for us, with my tiny, happy Clem tucked into his arms.

As I was unpacking boxes, savoring my new surroundings, and marveling at what God had done for us, I felt him nudge me. I heard him say, "This home isn't just for you. I want you to delight in it. I gave it to you because I love you. But one day soon I'm going to ask you to share it. Blessings are meant to be shared."

If I'm being honest, this terrified me. Because what else could God possibly mean other than that he wanted me to invite large groups of people to make s'mores with us in our fire pit and join us for brunch in our huge kitchen and come over on Saturday afternoons for a barbecue in our backyard pavilion? I realize that for a majority of people this sounds absolutely lovely, but for me, as an introvert, it made me feel like I couldn't breathe. I love hosting and being a hostess, but generally, I prefer that my guest list contain one name; maybe two, max.

What God was saying felt right, though. He had given us this extraordinary and wholly unexpected gift, and hoarding it felt wrong. Love given is meant to flow through us and into others. It's not meant to be greedily consumed and selfishly stockpiled. It's to be shared, so that it may take root in others where it can heal, strengthen, and nurture. And perhaps they, too, can pass it along. The nature of love—in fact, its essential purpose—is to grow and multiply and set the world on fire.

So I waited for God to inspire me with ways to share our new home with others. Though I did tell him that, unless some unusual and extreme situation demanded, I preferred to wait six months or so until our newest little one was born. Because me socializing is one thing, but me attempting to socialize while pregnant isn't something anyone needs in their life.

In December our Penelope was born. She had floppy ears like a bunny, which was not a thing I knew babies could have, being that she was our only baby to arrive a couple of weeks early. I think Dan found them so fetching that he secretly wished they would stay that way. But within days they perked up and looked normal, albeit particularly adorable. We brought her home a couple of weeks before Christmas.

The house was already lit with Christmas lights and the tree decorated haphazardly, which is really the best way for a tree to be decorated. We took pictures of Penelope under the tree and in Christmas stockings and wrapped in lights. I'm pretty sure that if you give birth to a baby in the weeks leading up to Christmas, these are things you are required to do. So we did. And I have no regrets about any of it.

The new year came, and Charleston experienced the most spectacular snowstorm. People debated whether this storm outdid the famous storm of 1989, which I couldn't weigh in on because I was only ten at that time and did not live in South Carolina. Either way, it was breathtaking.

Charleston is not a place that usually gets snow. So to have between five and seven inches fall around us was absolutely magical, and also lengthened the time of wonder that the birth of a new baby brings. We made ice ornaments and hung them from trees, built snowmen and snow-ladies and shared our clothes with them. We went on long walks in the woods and listened to the snow crunch under our boots. We put socks on our hands, because we only had seven mittens in total—none of which matched—and ten people. We made hot cocoa and cookies and took long bubble baths. We played music and games and wondered if we were dreaming.

When something magnificent like that happens, you tend to think that the year peaked early, that perhaps the good things that are coming won't be quite as good as the good things you have already experienced. I think maybe I had thought that. But I was wrong.

In late 2016, I had come across a YouTube video that was taking the world by storm. Two priests and a bishop made a carpool karaoke video to present at a youth conference. Little did they know that they would garner over six hundred thousand views in the blink of an eye. I watched it and was utterly charmed, and so I posted the following on my Facebook page: "It just became my #1 life goal to become friends with these priests. I have no other aspirations but this. The rest of my bucket list just got axed. Maybe I should send cookies?"[1]

I didn't end up sending the cookies, but I did invite one of the priests to my SiriusXM radio show. I can do these things because sometimes God can be crazy and gives incredibly private and introverted people radio shows. People like me who have no background in radio and never even thought about being on the radio until Lino Rulli showed up in their town and let them cohost his drive-time show on the Catholic Channel, which then opened up some really cool doors that God pushed them through.

And to make things even crazier, God created super smart

and inventive people who created things like my Comrex, a little black box that allows me to connect to a producer named Scott at the SiriusXM studios in Midtown Manhattan from my house. Given that I have eight children, it is really the only way any of this works. While my friend Jeannie Gaffigan and her husband, Jim, possess the kind of adventurous spirits that lead them to live in the city with a large family, I possess the sort that leads me to push strollers through quiet suburban neighborhoods . . . but only when traffic is at a minimum and everyone is on their best behavior.

Anyway, Father Kyle Manno accepted my invitation and I got to interview him, which was fantastic and fun. *What a lovely human being*, I thought afterward. *How delightful that he is now in my network. I should have him back on the show sometime.* So I did. Three more times, in fact. And somehow, through these interviews, even though Father Manno lives in Illinois and I live in South Carolina, a beautiful friendship began to take root. I looked back at the few text messages we exchanged in the beginning, trying to discover why and how it was that we grew so close so quickly, but there wasn't anything to explain it. It was just one of those God things.

In the summer of 2017, my friend Jen and I hosted our third Edel Gathering, a weekend-long conference for women of faith that involves sweet hotel rooms, sleeping-in-late mornings, hanging out by the pool, shopping for things you probably don't need, eating delicious food, drinking even more delicious wine, singing karaoke, dancing like crazy, and forming incredibly beautiful bonds with like-minded women.

The weeks leading up to Edel had been difficult. Jen and I had both faced spiritual turmoil, and practically speaking, it seemed like everything that could have gone wrong did. It was as if innumerable boxes filled with utter and complete chaos had fallen out of the sky and onto my head, one after another. All I could do was try to kick them to the side as quickly as possible to keep them in some sort of a semiorderly mess. And not die in the process.

This wasn't necessarily a surprise. It was actually pretty par for the course. Whenever anyone tries to bring something beautiful into the world, the attacks will come to throw them off track. It happens every time. But knowing they were coming—and would eventually pass—didn't make them any more fun to experience. I approached the first hours of the Edel event feeling a little heavy and wrung out.

But then, hours into the conference, a kind woman named Kathleen came over and gave me two gifts. One from her and one from Father Manno, whom she had met recently. During the next lull in the conference I sat down in our makeshift hotel office and opened the gifts. Inside Father Manno's gift was a letter and a collection of crucifix pendants that had been blessed by Pope Benedict.

When I read his letter, which was filled with words of encouragement and the promise of prayers, and opened his gift, which was so thoughtful and kind and perfect for me, I suddenly felt the weight and heaviness lift and peace like a river flow through me, just as the old hymn promised.

On the plane ride home, as I stared out the window at the clouds from over thirty thousand feet, I thought about all the things God had done that weekend and all the places he had shown up. He was there in the laughter and the silliness, the tears and the healing. Based on some of the karaoke performances that our attendees delivered, I'm pretty sure he took a few turns on the stage as well.

As I was thinking about Father Manno's gift and how it had set me back on track and infused me with hope and joy and the feeling of being loved, Penelope somersaulted in my womb. I knew at that moment that God had chosen Father Manno to be Penelope's godfather. It seemed crazy, given that we had never spoken outside of the radio show, and that Dan didn't know him at all. But it also felt strangely perfect, as God-ordained things always do.

Not only did he do us the honor of accepting our request to be Penelope's godfather, Father Manno also arranged to be at the baptism, which, given his busy priestly schedule, was not something I had expected or even dared to hope for. But there I was with my family at our perfect home in late January waiting for his arrival.

The kids were lined up outside, bubbling over with excitement to meet the priest they knew only through YouTube. Inside the house, I heard the squeals start from a distance and then move ever closer to the house. He came in wearing a Godfather Manno shirt with a picture of Penelope on it. It was as if we had known him for years. As if he belonged in our home. As if, in an instant, God had placed him in our hearts, and in some mystical way, made him a part of our family.

We spent three wonderful days with Father Manno, during which my kids almost killed him multiple times on the trampoline and Penelope became a child of God. Then he left to go back to his parish. Back to tend to his flock, to make them laugh and think, and to help them grow a little closer to God day by day. We missed him fiercely. But we knew he would return soon, because he was one of us now. Indeed, within weeks, another trip was scheduled, and again the joyful and impatient countdown began.

During the days following Father Manno's first visit, I realized that when God had told me he wished for us to share our home, he meant with Father Manno. "Let it be a place of retreat for him," I heard him say. "A place where the doors were always open and hugs were plentiful." That I could do. That I would, in fact, love to do. So I breathed the hugest sigh of relief, and God laughed at me because he loves me and delights in my ridiculousness.

One of the things God had given us in our incredible new home was a detached apartment that sits above the garage. We extended an invitation for Father Manno to stay there during his next visit, and he accepted, having determined that we were not strange or threatening, at least not terribly so. I then set about turning what was my office into a guest room.

I consulted Google and Pinterest and made a wonderful list of all the things a guest room might need. I gave bucketfuls of money to Target, and Target gave me presents because we're in love. That's how our relationship works. I hung pictures and fluffed pillows and made my son shampoo the carpets. I did all these things because I wanted Father Manno to feel at home when he came to visit. I wanted our home to be a place of rest and solace and comfort for him.

What I had been afraid to do in my home—invest in and pour my heart into it because we might one day have to leave it behind—I was doing to his guest room, even though Father Manno would definitely have to leave it behind. Standing a bit apart, a step or two removed from my own fears, I was able to see that goodness doesn't become any less good or valuable because it only lasts for a short time. In fact, if something is destined to be temporary, that is all the more reason to savor it while you have it.

It's a scary thing to put down roots and allow them to grow deep when you suspect that God might one day uproot you and ask you to start fresh somewhere new. Uprooting sounds like a painful thing, and in some ways change is always unsettling. But here's the thing about God: he is a master gardener who dearly loves you and all those roots he has helped you cultivate over the years. So if and when he does come and whisper that it's time for a transplant, he will oh-so-gently loosen your roots from the ground, tap away the excess dirt, support them in the palm of his hand, and carefully carry them to the new and wonderful place, where they will find fresh sustenance and different adventures.

My friend Sarah knew this. My children sensed it. And I'm slowly starting to learn it as well. Yes, there may be pain, a sense of loss, and a period of grieving for that which you must leave behind. But I think someone wise* once said that it is better to have loved and lost than never to have loved at all.

That is beginning to sound just about right to me.

---

*Probably Kanye, or maybe it was Alfred Lord Tennyson.

EIGHT

HIDDEN TREASURES

I long, as does every human being, to be at home wherever I find myself.

—Maya Angelou

Here is what I would remember always: the way he looked at her as if she were full of hidden treasures, treasures he couldn't wait to spend the rest of his life searching for; and the way she looked at him, too, like he was the most beautiful gift she had ever received, a gift she could not wait to explore and discover and taste.

They were newly married, just five weeks united. Adoring looks between newlyweds are not surprising, but what made them surprising for these two, to me anyway, was that five weeks ago was the first time they had laid eyes on each other. Theirs was a marriage arranged by their parents, the four people who loved them most in the world and wanted to give them the best chance at a happy and fruitful union. Their parents had not sought their input in the process.

An arranged marriage is not for everyone. It is not even for most people. Some would even say that it should not be for anyone. Once upon a time I might have said the same. But Anik and Neha, with their deep and sudden reverence for each other, changed my mind, or at least made me wonder whether I should reconsider my stance.

I met Anik and Neha at a party just months before I met Dan, and then dived headfirst into the biggest culture shock of my life by moving from the San Francisco Bay Area, where I had lived for seventeen years, to the Alabama Gulf Coast. The three of us hit it off immediately after meeting. When I think back on the few months we spent in friendship together, I am struck by just how profoundly people can leave their mark on you even though they might be in your life only for a short time. It has been almost two decades since I have spoken to them. Yet I still think about them from time to time, and I can see so clearly the little ways in which their influence informs my thoughts and actions.

After our first meeting, it didn't take long for us to fall into an easy routine of gathering at our favorite coffee shop, wandering the streets together, and then settling into the oversized couches that dotted their living room. The first place we ever met up was at a quiet Indian restaurant tucked down an even quieter alley in the heart of the city.

There were many things about that night that I remember. It was my favorite kind of San Francisco night, the kind that is so cool, damp, and foggy that you feel like you have been transported into another world in which everything is just a little bit softer and more consoling. The restaurant we had chosen was dimly lit and warm, with walls covered in rich tapestries. The votive candles on each table sparkled in the tiny mirrors that were woven into the tablecloths. And the chicken tikka masala was heavenly. Absolutely heavenly.

The chef had whipped into creation the perfect amalgamation of tomato and yogurt and coconut cream, cardamom and chilis and turmeric and coriander and paprika, onion and garlic and ginger. For me to crown this dish "perfect" is saying a lot, because I consider chicken tikka masala to be so delicious that I worry heaven won't feel quite complete without it. This is probably some form of heresy, but nevertheless, it remains my well-considered and staunch belief that God agrees with me and eats it at least once a week.

But it's not the fog or the atmosphere of the restaurant or even the chicken tikka masala that first comes to mind when I think about that night. It's Anik and Neha, and the fact that these two people, who had not chosen to be together, looked at each other with more hunger and curiosity and delight than any other newlywed couples I've ever had the good fortune to spend time with. Like so many things that I was wrong about before I knew better, it baffled me and made me feel a little off-balance.

I asked them about it. The wonder in their eyes, the love in their gestures, the peace that surrounded them as if they lived together, just the two of them, tucked in a dandelion. I hoped I had asked kindly and respectfully, but knowing myself as I do, I probably stumbled over the pebbles of my confusion and arrogance and misconceptions and ended up with a foot in my mouth. They were utterly open and unselfconscious, though, as if it had not occurred to them that what they were doing was completely countercultural and confusing to much of the world.

I remember Anik laughing wholeheartedly and saying, "But she is full of hidden treasures! She must be! Isn't everyone?" He then talked about how, to some degree, that was the thing most people miss when they consider or pass judgment on arranged marriages. The secret ingredient that pulls it all together, he said, was that he had no doubt this was true. That everyone has marvels and miracles woven within them. And he was determined to unearth every last one residing within his bride.

She laughed, too, clutching his hand, and said her mother had told her on the night before her wedding that Anik's flaws would quickly become obvious, that she would see them without any effort, and that her energy would be better spent ignoring them. But also that what would make their union transcendent was if she chose to spend her whole life seeking out and finding the wondrous things about him that no one else in the world would ever be able to see. From the freckle that sat hidden between the first and second toes on his left foot, to the way he would stop and share a hot meal with someone in need then swearing her to secrecy when she discovered this act of kindness, to the courage and fortitude he showed as he sat in his brokenness and strived to make peace with it. She was the only one in the entire world who would ever fully know and see and love his beauty. She was the only one whose breath would be stolen away by the innumerable unique and hidden pieces that made him unrepeatable.

I believe the same can be said for all marriages, at least

in potential. Everyone has basketfuls of loveliness hidden within them just waiting to be discovered by the curious besotted. Not knowing your betrothed before you walk down the aisle, Anik and Neha claimed, doesn't render this any less true.

I still would not choose an arranged marriage for myself or my children—though I would be lying if I did not admit to occasionally playing matchmaker over margaritas with friends—but these unions made more sense to me after our conversation. They demand a deep faith and trust in the idea that God has made every one of us good, that he has woven light into every human soul, and that, though it may sometimes get covered up a bit for a million different painful and tragic reasons, it never leaves. The light sits there just waiting to be discovered and uncovered, nurtured and adored, and for a lover to come along and demand with gentleness and adoration that it be put to good use. And that is an astoundingly fruitful way to approach romantic love, or any love for that matter.

To be open to encountering the world in this truth is such a beautiful way to live, in general, that I feel much gratitude toward Anik and Neha for revealing it to me. It has benefitted not only my relationships but also my search for rootedness, for home.

God arranges for us to live in certain places—in my case, quite a few different places—and these places may not always be the places we would have chosen had we been the ones doing the choosing. Nevertheless, there we are, standing in a new and unfamiliar land and feeling a little uncertain about the whole thing. If we are lucky, we might have a few friends already planted there and ready to help us find our footing. But sometimes there's no one. Sometimes it is just us and God and the promise of a big adventure.

If you had asked me fifteen years ago if I liked adventure, I would have responded with an emphatic yes! I imagined myself to be a Miss Rumphius of sorts, that fictional delight of a woman who sought to make the world more beautiful by planting lupines in the wild. I was ever hungry to pack my bags and see the world, to soak up what it had to teach me, to let it heal and invigorate me. And I would not have been wrong, had I taken the time to qualify my answer. To explain that, yes, I do love adventure, but only when the location is chosen by me, the date is selected by me, and all the other details are determined by my particular whims and wishes.

I backpacked through Europe for about a month the summer after I graduated from high school, and it was wonderful and surprising and enriching. But even then, with just a backpack, no cell phone to speak of, limited funds, and almost total autonomy, I still planned out my route ahead of time, made reservations at hostels after thorough research, and scheduled my dates of arrival and departure. I dotted my i's and crossed my t's. That's a wholly different kind of adventure than the one you face when God suddenly plucks you out of your comfort zone and drops you into an entirely new world that you may or may not feel is a good fit.

When God does that, when he answers my prayers for a life that is teeming with all sorts of surprises, challenges, and adventures, well, then he pretty quickly finds me turning to him with a look of exasperation on my face and telling him, "I didn't mean *this* sort of adventure." Yet he knows that, despite what I might say when I'm feeling intimidated and a little scared, these are precisely the sorts of adventures I long for.

Adventures that lift me up in the air and spin me around and, though they may disorient me and make me feel a bit dizzy for a time, in the end shake something loose inside me and leave me with far more clarity than I possessed when I began. Adventures that reveal parts of myself I didn't know existed or had simply forgotten they existed. Adventures that pull me eagerly far beyond the place where I find comfort, so that I have no choice but to stretch and grow and discover that my spirit is much stronger and more resilient than I had previously given credit. Adventures that turn me into a new creature of sorts, craving new experiences and asking new questions.

Sometimes I forget that these are the sorts of adventures I hope I will be able to say, when I look back at the end of my life, that I have experienced and embraced. I forget about the fruits and the epiphanies and the high of doing things I wasn't sure I could do. I forget about the metamorphosis born out of them.

Every time God came and gently lifted my roots out of the ground and transplanted them into new soil, in a new land, I curled up into a tight little ball and wondered to myself why everything couldn't have just stayed the same. Just for a little longer.

Every time I landed in a new place, I looked around and despaired at all the things that weren't what I had hoped they might be or were different from the things that made up my life in the past for which I still had great affection. I worried that the people and things that made up this new community wouldn't ever quite understand me or I them. That the grocery store wouldn't carry my favorite brand of yogurt or that my kids wouldn't be accepted and loved and embraced by their new friends the way they had been by their old. That I would forever be confused by the crisscrosses of overpasses and freeways and backroads. That it wouldn't rain as often or with as much force as my soul craves.

I worried that disorientation would become my new normal.

Almost a decade ago, in need of greater income, we walked through the only door that seemed open and moved from Alabama to Cincinnati, where Dan could teach at a small local college. Though moving to Alabama had been a culture shock at first, it eventually became a part of me and delighted my senses so much, with its lush greenery, wrap-around porches, and buttery magnolias, that I felt like I had lived there forever. To this day, I am sometimes surprised when I remember that I am not a native of the South.

Cincinnati was very different from Alabama. Not bad, just different in a way that felt especially strange and unknown to me. I cried the first night we were there and for many nights thereafter. I felt uncomfortable on its roads and with its people and in its places. It gave me a feeling of being oddly exposed, of standing out like the strawberry that finds its way into the blueberry basket at the farmers market. Only not as lovely. I felt like that poor, moldy little strawberry that everyone wrinkles their noses at before quickly moving on to another fresher basket. I stayed home far more than was good for me. Far more than was good for anyone.

Then I remembered Anik and Neha. I always thought of them during times of change and periods of adjustment.

Sometimes not for months, and only after wallowing for a bit. But always eventually. I remembered how their entire marriage was oriented toward discovering the hidden treasures within each other, and I thought that maybe, just maybe, I might be able to do the same in this new home that still felt so unknown and ill-fitting, even after all these months. I thought that perhaps I could be curious about it instead of afraid of it.

So I forced myself to venture out more. I took short adventures to familiar places that followed me wherever we moved. Like IHOP, with its scrumptious cheese blintzes. And Barnes & Noble, with its stacks of books wrapped in beautiful, enticing covers. And movie theaters, with their buttery popcorn and sticky floors.

Somehow, ever so slightly, those tentative baby steps piqued my curiosity about my new home, leading to bigger, bolder steps. Steps that took me to nature preserves, where I watched my children climb on trees and wade in streams and pet baby farm animals. To a running path that breathed life back into me. And to a splash pad that entertained my kids for hours, allowing me to get lost in chick lit. Even though I was over two thousand miles away from Northern California, these things reminded me of that home and made me feel less adrift.

Then one morning I realized that all these steps I had taken—both the tentative and the bold—left me feeling a little less out of place and a little more at home. This is not to say, exactly, that I woke up and thought, *Oh, I was wrong! I do fit in here after all!* But that I had found things to which I could cling, things that made me feel less unmoored, things that brought me solace in a place that had long felt hostile, though surely it didn't mean to. These things helped me to remain there for as long as God willed.

It's funny how you can think God is preparing you for one thing, only to discover later that it was but the smallest piece of the puzzle. At the time, I thought he merely wanted me to make peace with the fact that my address changed so frequently, but in retrospect, I can see that his plan was much more vast and more brilliant. He was teaching me how to adjust, to pivot, to flow, to not be so rigid in my thinking and life, and to force myself to adapt to new situations when all I want to do is resist with all my might.

I traveled to India with my father when I was in high school to tour the country and visit the tomb of a spiritual guru named Meher Baba, who was beloved by my hippie parents. Our pilgrimage didn't last long, just a couple of weeks, if that. But that brief sojourn changed me. It remains within me, informing me of who I am and how I see the world. After days wandering past and among the poorest of the poor, my heart became more tender toward those in need—though not nearly tender enough. The vibrant colors of the saris and the bolts of fabric stacked to the ceiling in hidden stores tucked down long, ribbonlike alleyways permanently destroyed my penchant for black and influence my decorating choices to this day. I still crave lassi and samosas and, of course, chicken tikka masala almost constantly. Even a random conversation I had with another pilgrim about the art of writing—a love we discovered we shared while sitting on the front porch of our hotel—pops up from time to time as I'm crafting sentences.

This is what places and the people we meet in those places, even the most transitory, are meant to do. They are meant to descend on us and shape us and help us evolve. To leave indelible marks of color and insight and newly discovered loves and passions all over our souls. To stretch and broaden and change us. To enliven us. To make us hungry.

I have a friend who travels for work to countries all over the world approximately six months out of the year. And he hates it, or at least he did in the beginning. Now he does that thing I don't always do very well and makes the most of it. Though he is every bit as much of a homebody as I am, he looks around at his life and his job and has faith that he is exactly where God wants him to be, even if that is away from his home and bed and favorite chair for 182.5 days out of every year. He takes each day one at a time, asking God each morning to reveal what he is meant to gather from this new place.

When I told him, years ago, of my struggle to adapt to change and my hunger for rootedness, he smiled and said,

> That's probably because you're limiting your understanding of rootedness. I have my primary home, my favorite home, the one in which the people I love most in the world live. The place where I feel most secure and nurtured. But if I see home as a place where I find shelter and am fed and maybe expand my horizons and learn a little about myself in the process, I have transient homes all over the world that I visit frequently. Perhaps that is not how everyone understands home, but it is how I have come to understand it, and this way of thinking has brought me a lot of

peace during a season that looks different than I might have hoped.

After talking to him, I began to wonder, What if the key to rootedness is less about staying in one place and more about feeding yourself with the things that will make your roots strong and healthy? What if it is about immersing yourself in whatever town or country or continent God places you and, with curiosity, soaking up whatever that place may have to teach you? What if it is about encountering things you have never encountered before and letting them show you where you have been wrong, letting them open your eyes and your heart, and letting them heal you? What if it is about eating good food and reading magnificent books and absorbing soul-stirring works of art? What if it is about allowing disappointment and heartache and a sense of being displaced to reveal to you the depths of God's love? What if it is even about, in some mystical way, leaving a little part of yourself behind to unite you to the place?

Because I think the key to rootedness might be about all of that. And if this is true, then our potential to feel rooted is limitless and not remotely determined by or dependent on the circumstances of our living situation. This is such happy news for those of us who are standing knee deep in a life that looks a lot different from the one we might have imagined.

Maybe all we've ever needed is to look around at our surroundings, however strange and unsettling they may at first seem, and then laugh, just like Anik, and say, "But she is full of hidden treasures! She must be! Isn't everyone?"

NINE

GIVEN

Everybody has a home team: it's the people you call when you get a flat tire or when something terrible happens. It's the people who, near or far, know everything that's wrong with you and love you anyway. . . . These are the ones who tell you their secrets, who get themselves a glass of water without asking when they're at your house. These are the people who cry when you cry. These are your people, your middle-of-the-night, no-matter-what people.

—Shauna Niequist

When I was in my early twenties, I knew an old woman named Mrs. Ainsley. She wore summer dresses paired with wool knee socks and sandals and had long grey hair that she twisted into two braids and then pinned up on top of her head. She was odd and wonderful and honest in a way that made me love and fear her in equal parts. She was the kind of woman who would pat you on the hand, gaze at you affectionately, and say, "Well, my goodness, you seem to have developed quite a penchant for pie, haven't you?"

After a few moments of trying to sort out whether she had really just thrown all generally accepted rules of etiquette out the window and was saying what I thought she was saying (she was), I would stammer out something along the lines of, "Well, yes, I suppose I have, but only because everything is so hard right now. My marriage is struggling and the bills aren't being paid and my baby doesn't sleep and I feel scared and pie makes it all go away. At least for a moment." She would then resume patting my hand and invite me to tell her more.

Loneliness reminds me of Mrs. Ainsley.

Without people in your life, there are no parties to go to, no phone calls to make, no café to visit. There's a lot of silence. You try to drown out that silence with music and Netflix and endless streams of social media, but you always end up in the same spot: alone with your thoughts and God. So you start talking to him—about everything. You tell him your ideas for books you want to write and corners you're thinking of decorating differently. You ask for his opinion about dinner. "Beef bourguignon or broccoli cheese soup?" Soup? Yes, that was exactly what you were leaning toward too. You give him your opinion about mosquitoes, and then ask, not to criticize but merely out of curiosity, "Do you ever have any regrets about that creative decision? Because, just between me and you, that's a hard one to understand."

Then, somewhere between the babbling about decorating

and dinner, you hear God whisper, "But what about the sadness, beloved? Tell me about that."

Ah, yes. That.

So you and God begin the work of digging deep, dragging out all of the ugliness within, and dealing with it. Why do you hurt and where do you need healing? Where are you going and what are you running from? Who do you want to become and when are you going to take that next step?

For me, if I'm willing to lean in and not fight it too much, this is the fruit of loneliness. It strips me of all the silliness, distractions, and things of the world that are beautiful and good until I use them to anesthetize myself. It makes me face the things that I don't want to face. Just like Mrs. Ainsley.

I went through a long season of loneliness shortly after I was married. Within a period of a couple of years, we'd moved three times and started a family. All things, for all their goodness, caused profound evolutions in my faith life and left me feeling somewhat disoriented and unmoored.

At the time, Dan was working full-time and going to school full-time, so I was often left alone. And having not yet replenished my supply of local friends and drowning in young motherhood, I was truly alone.

Time alone is not something I mind too much in and of itself. It suits my introversion well. Particularly during this season, socialization wasn't what I needed at the end of a long day—the latest of long days in a string of long days and even longer sleepless nights—but rather baths and books and blessed silence.

After a while, though, right around the time my third

child and first daughter was still so new that sniffing her fuzzy head brought on an immediate high, the difference between having a friend and having a close, trusted friend started to become a source of pain. Dan has always been a willing listener, but he's not a woman or a mother or a wife. He will forever be one chromosomal X removed from my life experience.

I needed someone who could tell me that I wasn't alone, that she experienced and thought and felt the same things I did, and that I wasn't crazy, or if I was, that it was a good kind of crazy she knew well. I wanted a friend who wasn't afraid to call me out when I was behaving badly or possibly struggling under spiritual attack. The kind of friend who wouldn't blink if I admitted that I'd cyber stalked someone, eaten a bucket of chicken, or just spent my entire grocery budget at Sephora, but instead would ask what I discovered, how it tasted, and if I purchased anything amazing. A friend who would then take me by the hand and gently guide me out of my insanity and back to a place of peace and wholeness.

I'd grown up with an amazing tribe of friends, but we'd lost touch after I moved across the country. This was probably more my fault than theirs. I'd gone through seismic changes in my life that none of my childhood friends had undergone—in just three years, I'd converted to Christianity, gotten married, and become a mother—and so I wasn't sure how to maintain our relationships, standing as I was in such a different world from theirs. Still, it seemed to me that if we could gather and hug and talk face-to-face, we could find new ways to relate to one another and bring forth a new season of friendship. But the distance felt too much to bridge, so I quietly walked away.

I missed the intimacy of those friendships that were forged through sixteen years of joys, tragedies, and shared experiences. This was part of the reason I was desperate to find a place to put down roots. Friendships such as these, it seemed to me, were the fruit of sizable investments of energy, vulnerability, and time. They were born of a commitment to a community that wasn't fleeting or temporary. If I wanted to re-create the kind of friendships I'd lost, my family and I needed to stay put in the heart of Texas, put our stake in the ground and build a life. And then I needed God to send me that person, the Anne to my Diana.

So I asked. Then I waited. For what felt like a very long time, I waited.

The nice thing about God is that he meets you where you are. People forget this sometimes. I forget this often. I think that I have to get it all together, overcome my addictions and vices, and become a little more like Mother Teresa and a little less like me before God will step into my life and help. Worthiness first, God later.

I remember hearing a popular preacher once say, "God helps his friends, so if you want help, you had better stay in his good graces." This was shortly after my conversion to Christianity, and all I knew then was that this man was incredibly well respected and had been at this Christianity thing for a lot longer than I had, so I figured I should probably listen to him. But instead of inspiring me to embrace a greater level of holiness, his words made me feel hopeless. Every time I would stumble and fall, choosing vice over virtue, or simply come face-to-face with my own humanness, my heart would sink. I would imagine God up in heaven dispassionately shaking his head and saying to his angelic secretary, "Nothing to be done about this one. Write her out of the will until she can get her act together. Close the floodgates of love."

For years I carried around this belief. For years I believed that because I didn't love God enough—clearly I didn't, for if I did, I would behave better—he wouldn't help me. God wouldn't console me when I was sad. He wouldn't guide me when I was lost. He wouldn't provide for me when I needed assistance. He wouldn't love me. After all, who would want to be in a relationship with a person who takes all the love you give them, devours it hungrily, and then only gives a small portion of it back?

Well, God does, as it turns out.

I once shared with a friend some seemingly insurmountable financial problem I was facing and expressed how hopeless everything felt. She responded by telling me that I should go to God and ask him for help. I paused for a moment and then said, with tears in my eyes, "I would, but I don't love him enough for him to help me." I was so hard on myself in those days that I couldn't see that I was simply a young, exhausted mother trying her best. I could only see my failures.

She looked at me sadly and said, "But that's not how it works, Hallie. That's not how it works."

She was right. That isn't how it works. We don't generate love; God does. We're not perfect; God is. And within God's perfect, eternal love is an ocean of mercy that expresses itself in endless compassion. He helps us not because we're his friends (though we are) or because we've behaved particularly well (usually we haven't), but simply because he's utterly and completely enamored with us.

As an aside, years later, that preacher who said God only helps his friends became embroiled in a very public and heartbreaking scandal and disappeared. Sometimes I think of him and wish I could give him a hug and say, "God still loves you, you know. More than you can imagine." And I want to tell him, lovingly, of course, that he got it wrong. That, just as my friend insisted, his understanding of God is not how God works. God wades right into our storms and ugliness, into all of our failures and mistakes, with his hand outstretched, knowing that it is usually at those moments that we can see him best and are most willing to grasp his hand and let him help and love us.

So it was, on the day I decided to take God's outstretched hand after pleading for a friend. I'd been at the motherhood thing in the heart of Texas for five years, the Christianity and marriage thing for seven, and I didn't feel that I was doing any of it well, or even halfway decently. After years of struggling, largely and foolishly fueled by the force of my own pathetic will, I found myself down for the count. My life showed all the signs of someone who'd given up. Clutter built up all around me, passions neglected, meals uninspired, exercise nonexistent, yoga pants beloved. My lust for life was nowhere to be found.

I'd just put my three little ones down for a nap and was catching up on blog reading when I spotted something interesting. There, right toward the top of one of my favorite blogs, was a picture of the interior of my parish. The woman who penned the blog, Jennifer Fulwiler, had taken it on the day she'd been received into the church, which meant . . . she was local. I also found out that she, too, had three children under the age of six. So I wondered if she might be experiencing the same insanity. Maybe we had a lot in common. Like that we were both converts and introverts and had lots of little ones. Maybe she'd like to get together sometime. Then it occurred to me that I could send her an email and tell her we belong to the same parish. Before I had a chance to consider whether such an enthusiastic email from a desperate-sounding complete stranger might make her consider getting a restraining order, I typed it up and pressed Send.

She didn't call the police, which I considered a solid first step toward friendship. Instead, she wrote back and asked if I wanted to meet up.

C. S. Lewis once said that friendship "is born at the moment when one man says to another 'What! You too? I thought that no one but myself . . .'"[2]

This is how it was for Jennifer and me. In some ways we were as different as two people could be—the night owl (Jen) and the early bird (me), the lover of a glass of fine wine and nonfiction (Jen) and the ice cream and chick lit aficionado (me). I love to ride bikes, and Jen claims that one day she'll drive by me in a limo and shout out, "Get a car!" as she raises her glass of champagne in my direction and blows me a kiss. But in all the most important ways, we finished each other's sentences.

It took a few months for us to take our relationship from

acquaintance to "I'll cut anyone who ever tries to mess with you" level. Not because of a lack of instant connection but because of our mutual chaotic circumstances. It was a wonder we could even find the words to introduce ourselves, as sleep-deprived as we were. Once we got our momentum going, though, we were all in.

Most of the time, our friends see only one side of us. Friends who know us on a spiritual level see us when we are contemplating God and the deeper things of life. Friends who know us professionally are familiar with our career aspirations and talents. There are also the friends we call when we need to get out of the house, have a drink, and lay down some truths about everyone who is ruining our lives and might possibly be trying to kill us. There are the fitness friends, the school parent friends, the writing workshop friends, the neighborhood friends—all are valuable, and all fill an important role in our lives.

Almost immediately, Jen was all of these things rolled into one gorgeous, six-foot-tall redhead. She got me. She knew how to make sense of all my seemingly incongruous pieces that make me me. Though we'd known each other only a short while, it was really weird to think that there was ever a time when she wasn't in my life.

We started talking daily, often multiple times a day, just to check in, say hello, or report back on some development (or catastrophe) in our lives. One of my favorite early memories of us occurred after we had been teasing each other about our wildly different approaches to romance.

"You are going to be so proud of me, Hallie," she said on the phone.

"Hey, Jen. Why am I going to be proud of you?"

"Well, you know how you're always trying to convince Joe and me to have stay-at-home date nights because sitters are so expensive—"

"And getting ready for sitters strips you of your will to live? Yes, I remember."

"So we did it! We had an at-home date night last night!"

"That's awesome! Did you drag your mattress downstairs and into the living room and build a fort?" This was my idea of a fun time, but I knew it wasn't Jen's.

"No, you insane person. We're never going to do that. We did something even better. Guess!" Jen's playful personality was contagious.

"Um . . . you climbed on top of your roof with a bottle of wine and stargazed?"

"I think you would know if I was calling you from the hospital, Hallie. No. We created spreadsheets!"

I was temporarily stunned into silence. "Sexy spreadsheets?"

"Um . . . no? I mean, maybe? We worked on our five- and ten-year plans."

My exhausted brain could not compute what she was saying. "How is that a date night, Jen?"

"Well, we made cocktails and we were together and we did something we both love. Isn't it obvious?"

I laughed, congratulated her, and, having just spotted Jack and Daniel (my four- and five-year-olds) attempting to parachute off our six-foot fence, quickly hung up.

For the first time in many years, I started to feel my loneliness abate. Though I could see the fruits of the years of solitude I had just walked through, I was deliriously happy that God was leading me into a new season—and stupidly assumed that he wouldn't give me such a gift just to take it away.

I figured that Jen and I had a multitude of mornings sitting on the soccer field sidelines, delivering dinners to each other on hard days, and carpooling in our future. I pictured myself calling her at the end of long days and telling her to meet me for margaritas in fifteen minutes. I thought she would occasionally spot me on my bike, roll down her window, and give me a hard time.

I was wrong.

Our years in Texas had been brutal. I'd really believed that if we could just get to Texas (not an easy feat given our lack of resources and the cost of moving), we would be home. And meeting Jen sealed the deal. But something about our being there didn't fit.

For one thing, there was no rain. At least not during the years we inhabited the Lone Star State. Dan and I love rain. The way most people feel on sunny days is how we feel on rainy days. Like everything is right with the world. And realistically, there was no work to be found; or rather, what work there was, it was insufficient to support our growing family. For three years we struggled to make ends meet. Dan often worked two jobs while in school just to pay the bills and put food on the table. We fought, we made up, we struggled, and we prayed and prayed and prayed. But all we found was dearth. Eventually, we were forced to ask ourselves whether God might be leading us to make a change. Telling us to go back to Alabama where Dan could work at the family vacuum cleaner business, at least until we got back on our feet.

Everything inside me resisted admitting what felt like defeat. I was convinced that if we could hold on for just one month more, and then one month more, the rain would return, and we would find relief, and we could stay. I hated the thought of leaving my family and couldn't bear the thought of losing Jen. As inseparable as we had so quickly become, I had seen distance put a quiet end to friendships. If even those I'd nurtured for sixteen years could end, what would it do to a friendship still so young?

I tried to deny the upcoming move and didn't tell her right away. But while the kids and I were hanging out at Jen's house, God opened a door for me to share the news.

"So there's this camp I'm thinking of sending Donnell and Lane to this summer. Do you think Jack and Daniel would want to join them?" Jen asked. She had placed a pizza in the middle of her dining table, then turned around to fill sippy cups while I distributed the slices.

Anxiety bubbled up inside me. I'd been dreading sharing our decision with her for weeks, uncertain what her response would be. I didn't think she'd be angry, but I wasn't sure I had the emotional bandwidth to handle her sadness or the subtle dismissal from her life that seemed inevitable. Not because she was the type to dismiss people, but because, surely, she could see the writing on the wall as I could. We would promise to stay in touch and make vague plans to visit, but life would get in the way, and slowly the physical distance between us would manifest itself relationally. This was part of the reason I never made much of an attempt to develop friendships back when we were in Alabama. Since I didn't envision us staying there long term, I didn't want to bond with people only to lose them.

"Unfortunately, I don't think we're going to be here," I said.

"What do you mean? Are you guys going on vacation?"

I continued cutting the pizza into small bites for the little ones and took a deep breath. "No, it looks like we're moving back to Alabama."

She paused, and in that pause I felt all the terribleness I'd imagined hurtling toward me. "Oh, wow."

"I know. I'm so sorry. This sucks. We've tried everything we can think of to make this work, but we're just hitting wall after wall. The only thing we can think to do is to go back to Alabama and regroup. Dan can work at the family business while he looks for work as a teacher, and I don't know, I guess we'll just figure it out as we go."

"You don't need to apologize, Hallie. You have to do what's best for your family. I totally get that. God has a plan for your family, and you have to follow him. I'll miss days like these, but it's not like we're not going to stay in touch. We communicate more through email and over the phone anyway. It's going to be fine. You'll see."

But in the silence that hung between us, I was pretty sure we both knew that fine was the opposite of what it would be.

One month later we were back in Alabama, and as I was trying in vain to force our many sundry items into our new, very cozy home, I heard the phone ring.

"Dan! Have you seen the box with our cast-iron skillets inside?" I called, ignoring the insistent buzzing.

"I think they're still in the garage. Hey, I think Jen is calling again. Do you want me to answer?"

"No, I'll call her back later."

"Too late. I already picked up." He handed me the phone and walked out to the garage in search of our skillets.

"Hey, Jen," I said with a sigh.

"Where on earth have you been? I've been calling you for days. I was worried that you'd fallen into a Louisiana swamp on your way to Alabama and had been eaten by alligators."

"Ha. No. It just took us a couple of days to get our phone connected, and I've been having trouble with my cell phone signal. Everything is really chaotic right now."

"Oh, okay. Well, I'm glad that's done because I have five million things to tell you. Most importantly, CVS isn't carrying my favorite hair gloss anymore. What are we going to do about this?"

I laughed, and then immediately felt guilty for lying to her about the phone service. I realized I was protecting my heart and needed to embrace that I missed her. Just as I knew I would miss her as soon as I heard her voice, which is why I'd been avoiding her calls. I'd never been able to relate to people who prefer not to say goodbye before leaving their loved ones for a long period of time, but now I understood. I didn't want a long, painful process of growing apart, which I believed was inevitable. I just wanted to rip the Band-Aid off. I was starting to see, though, that Jen wasn't giving up on our friendship, and, though I still had my fears and doubts, I loved her even more for it.

That was eight years ago. Just a moment ago my doorbell

rang and there on the welcome mat sat a package from Jen. Inside was a large bottle of mead. Why would she send me mead? "Because, Hallie, it's the nectar of the gods, obviously. I don't know how we're still friends when you've never even tasted mead."

Of the nine years we've been friends, we only lived in the same town for a few months. And even though our connection during that time was instant and strong, it was only a hint of the depth of the friendship that we would develop from across four states. One of my daughters is her goddaughter and one of hers is mine. We've cried together, laughed together, and plotted revenge together. We've survived hospital stays, a devastatingly sick newborn, and a heartbreaking miscarriage. We've shared our fears and our failures and our wildest dreams. We even founded a women's conference together.

Yet rarely were we breathing the same air as we did all these things.

She's my girl. My sister. My partner in crime. My ride or die. How silly of me to put limitations on a God who is known for parting seas and multiplying loaves.

For a long time, I told myself that once I had my life perfectly in order, I would find friends. Lock down life first, friends later. But what I'd missed was that some friendships are so extraordinary, so ordained by God, that they transcend the limitations of a chaotic existence. In fact, in many ways, these people become your port. They protect you from storms and give you a safe haven in which to rest. It is to them that you can reveal the ugliest parts of yourself, knowing that they will still welcome you even if you can't seem to let go of those lesser, shameful pieces of your being, at least not right away. They feed you and nourish you and heal you when you are sick. They laugh with you and love you no matter the distance that separates you.

Saint Pope John Paul II once wrote a meditation on "givenness" that is breathtakingly profound. I remember being struck by these opening words in particular when I first read them:

> Can one man say to another, "God has given you to me"? As a young priest, I once heard my spiritual director say to me: "Perhaps God wills to give that person to you." These were words of encouragement, urging me to trust God and accept the gift one man becomes for another. I suspect it didn't immediately dawn on me that these words also hide a profound truth about God, man, and the world. The world, the very world in which we live, the human world . . . is the setting of an ongoing exchange of gifts—gifts given and received in many different ways. People live not only alongside one another, but also in manifold relationships. They live for each other; relating to one another, they are brothers and sisters, wives and husbands, friends, teachers, students. . . . It may seem that there is nothing extraordinary in this; it is just the normal pattern of human life. In certain places, this pattern intensifies, and it is there, at those points of "intensification," that this gift of one person for another becomes most real.[3]

I met a young mother named Maggie at a conference I spoke at recently. Maggie felt frustrated by the fact that

God was not allowing her to use her artistic gifts during this season of her life. She couldn't understand why he had given her such a hunger to create but not the things she needed to pursue her passions—sleep, childcare, financial stability, opportunity. She asked me if I knew the reason. I thought for a moment, then said, "Space. He's creating space within you."

God has such a desire to fill us with good things, but first he has to create the space within us to receive them. The years of loneliness that I experienced before I met Jen were not purposeless. God wasn't just asking me to twiddle my thumbs and hang out for a while because he was running behind schedule. He was preparing me for the gift of a friendship, for this "intensification" that Pope John Paul II spoke of, that would not only last a lifetime but would require me to stretch myself and be vulnerable and accept the love and give of myself to another.

We are not meant to portion out parts of ourselves to the people God brings into our lives. We are meant to love them wholly and wildly as Jesus loves us. God knew that in order for my friendship with Jen to take root and grow in ways that are healthy and strong and life giving, I needed time to ready myself and allow him to ready me for it.

I told Maggie that I suspected he was doing the same with her. God wasn't saying that now that she had become a mother she had to deny her own desires and aspirations—just as he wasn't consigning me to a life of loneliness. He was simply asking her to submit and surrender to a season of preparation so that when the time came, she would have the space needed to receive whatever particular gifts he wants to pour into her, and then, after having received his gifts, she can go forth and share them with the world.

As I meditated on this concept of God creating space within us, I realized that just as Maggie can take her artistic gifts with her wherever she goes because they live in the space God has created within her, I, too, can take my friendship with Jen anywhere God leads me because, in some mystical way, she lives within me, as do all the people God gives me. Though a great many miles may forever separate us, I never had anything to fear.

Jen dwells in me, and I dwell in her. We're not always well behaved. Sometimes our dwelling place gets a little messy, and I imagine that she occasionally wants to evict me. But it's a little hard to return a present from God.

I'm sorry, Jen, but I'm afraid you're stuck with me.

TEN

BEAUTIFUL GIRLS

Unless you are willing to do the ridiculous,
God will not do the miraculous.

—Mother Angelica

For a long time I thought I wanted to live on a farm. I imagined that I would be perfectly suited for such a romantic life. I dreamed of picking apples and strawberries and peaches and holding them afloat in my apron. Baking pies and then eating them while perched on white picket fences beneath a big blue sky. Cuddling piglets. Turning soil and tucking seeds and smelling the earth on my body, which, I pictured, was incredibly toned and attractive in this fantasy because of all the farmwork I attended to each day. Reviving myself by biting into a warm tomato and letting the juice drip down my chin. Wildflowers. Everywhere wildflowers.

Things that did not make it into this vision: backbreaking labor, mice, biting bugs, rising before the sun, slaughter and the circle of life, failed crops, financial fears, spotty internet connections, and the fact that I don't like the taste of raw tomatoes.

Another story I like to tell myself is that I wish I could live in a neighborhood just like the one my late grandparents, Opa and Nama, lived in while I was growing up.

When I was young, my mom, sister, and I used to fly out to Richardson, Texas, every summer to spend two weeks with them. Each morning started the same way. Either Opa or Nama would slide their feet into their slippers, don their robe, and step out into the front yard to retrieve the paper. Almost every day they would encounter one of their neighbors, who was also retrieving the paper or taking a walk or watering the lawn as the sun peeked over the roofs. They would stop for a moment to say hello before returning to the kitchen for breakfast. I don't know why these particular details of those summer days stick in my mind so happily, but they do.

In the midst of yet another one of our many moves, I remember sharing this memory with Dan and telling him that I would love to find a neighborhood just like that. He laughed, as he does when I tell him something utterly ridiculous, and said, "Hallie. You would absolutely hate that."

"What are you talking about? I would so totally love that."

He laughed again. "And when people knock on the door, are you still going to hide and threaten the children with bodily harm if they make a sound?"

I laughed too, because he wasn't wrong.

I stand with both feet firmly planted right on that thin line that separates the introverts from the cave-dwelling hermits. If I didn't have all these children with all their inexplicable social needs, I could decorate the heck out of a cave and reside there quite happily. It's possible that I'd invite people to my cave. I like people. I do. I just need them to schedule their visits far in advance, so I have adequate time to prepare. You can't just show up and knock on someone's door. That would be insane.

One of the commonly held misconceptions about introverts, even extreme introverts like myself, is that we don't like people. I get this. If you and I have an amazing conversation at a party and then you suggest that we get together sometime and it takes me several months to make that happen, it's only fair that you might wonder if I have people issues. The truth, though, is that I love people. I love hearing their stories and seeing all the quirks that make them unique. I love hugging and laughing and sharing heartbreaks and struggles and tears. I love the feeling of connection that can occur when you reveal yourself to people with complete vulnerability and then they reveal themselves right back. It's just that, at the end of the day, I find it exhausting, which is not a bad thing. I simply need a lot of downtime to recharge my batteries.

Hence Dan's accurate statement that I would hate to live in a neighborhood with neighbors who are, as neighbors should be, neighborly.

I know this about myself, so it's interesting that I thought, even for a second, that I might desire to live in the kind of social community where people interact with one another prior to having their morning coffee. That is not a thing I would ever want to do. But something about it called to me. And usually when crazy things call to me, those things are actually the hidden voice of God giving me a nudge and telling me to pay attention, to dig a little deeper.

So I dug, and what I unearthed was a hunger inside myself for a tribe. Not the kind of tribe, mind you, that is in any way communal, but a tribe nonetheless. One that could look at my uncommon life with all these little ones (six at the time) and tell me that I wasn't alone. That they, too, often had to say their morning prayers kneeling on the bathroom floor, and sometimes lying prostrate on the cold tile in utter exhaustion, because it was the only place where they could find a moment of solitude. That they, too, understood how I could so fiercely love my children who also made me want to pull out my hair. And that they, too, wondered whether their children were destined to end up in jail or as canonized saints, two options that somehow strangely seemed equally possible.

But it had to be a long-distance tribe, because I just couldn't be tribe-ing it up all day every day. I needed to tribe only at very specific and occasional times. I needed to live in a highly controlled tribe environment, at least at that particular moment in my life. And so I told all of this to God.

Sometimes God listens to me ramble on and say absurd things, and then very kindly replies with an, "Um, no, because that is insane." But sometimes, most of the time even, he responds with, "Still insane, Hallie, but, you know, maybe we could make this work if we're very creative. And if you're willing to do some equally crazy things to make it happen."

Because here's a secret: God loves ridiculous dreams and crazy plans. People think God loves prudence, and he does, and it has its place for sure, but I believe God loves dreamers who get wild ideas and take insane leaps of faith even more. Can't you just see him rubbing his hands together with a mischievous twinkle in his eyes every time someone comes to him with one of those wild ideas, and saying, "Yeah, yeah, yeah. This could work. Let's do this thing"? I can. Most of the time I think we're the ones who end up putting on the breaks. But not God—that is, as long as your dreams are aligned with his will. He's ready to go if you are.

Another person who likes to dream big, crazy dreams is Jen. She always has about fifty thousand ideas percolating in her brain at once, and I fear that if for some inexplicable reason those things went away, she would literally wither and die. Sometimes she calls me up and, with more enthusiasm than a kitten who has caught her first mouse, starts pouring all of them into my head. Then I would have to go take a very long nap because my brain shorted out just by listening to her talk about all these mad, brilliant ideas of hers.

Case in point: In 2013, Jen and I gave birth to baby boys less than a week apart. Twenty-two weeks into her pregnancy, Jen's doctors discovered that she had life-threatening bilateral pulmonary embolisms. She spent weeks in the hospital and underwent a variety of surgeries that, were they not necessary to save her life, would never be allowed under the statutes of the Geneva Convention. Then she experienced an extremely traumatic birth. Just hours after her son made his way into the world, he was swept away to the NICU, where he would stay for several weeks due to multiple holes in his lungs.

She is a superhero, basically.

A couple of months after her son was finally able to come

home and she had recovered, at least partially, Jen called me and laid more insanity in my lap.

"Hey, Hallie."

"Mmmm."

"Are you there?"

"Mmmmhmm."

"Why aren't you talking like a normal human being?"

"Because Charlie woke up twenty-four times last night and I'm too exhausted to employ the English language."

"That's funny."

"No, I'm serious. I'll send you a screenshot of my Fitbit sleep tracker. Twenty-four times!"

"Whoa. Anyway, I was thinking—"

"What's that like, Jen?"

"You know how we've talked about organizing a women's conference? I think it might be time."

"Are you insane? Never mind. Don't answer that, because I already know the answer. Just listen. We both just had babies. You almost died. Your son spent weeks in the NICU. I have a baby who hates sleep. And you want us to start a conference?"

"I just think it's time, Hallie, and I'm pretty sure God agrees with me."

"Then you're both insane. But fine. Tell me about this conference you want to create."

"I don't know. I didn't say I had any details yet. That's why I'm calling!"

So there I was on one side of the phone in South Carolina and she on the other in Texas, and we thought, simultaneously and in silence, about this theoretical conference. Then God did that thing he does where he pulls things out of thin air and places them right inside your brain, and you start to suspect, with a distinct sense of foreboding, that he was indeed up to something.

"Okay, Jen, here's what I'm thinking. Have you seen that movie *Beautiful Girls* starring Timothy Hutton? There's this scene in it where his character is in a bar with a bunch of friends and they spontaneously gather around the piano and start singing 'Sweet Caroline.' Gosh, it's such a great scene. Anyway, I think, were we to host a conference, that's the vibe I'd want. That sense of camaraderie and belonging and support."

Jen started choking on her coffee. "You did not just seriously say that, Hallie."

"Um, yes, I did. Why? Do you hate that movie or something?"

"No. But Hallie, that is the exact same scene that God just placed in my mind."

"*What?*"

"I'm serious. It just popped into my head. I didn't even know you'd seen that movie!"

I'd like to say that it was right at that moment that we knew a conference had been born. But we were just sane enough to grasp that, despite this crazy moment of providence, putting on a conference was a ridiculous and probably foolish idea. So we came up with a plan. We would both get off the phone and call our husbands at work and pitch the proposal to them. If they thought it was a good idea, which they wouldn't, thank goodness, we would proceed.

Here is what we told them: we had come up with this idea for a conference that would require large amounts of time, lots of energy, huge sacrifices on their part, and a not insignificant financial risk. And by "not insignificant," we were talking about nearly one hundred thousand dollars, and neither of us were (or are) wealthy, or even financially stable, really.

One thing Jen and I have in common is that we are both married to very wise, strong, self-confident men. I took comfort in this, because it meant that we would not have to create and host a conference. Dan isn't stupid; he recognizes bad ideas when he sees them, and he isn't afraid to pull me back from the brink of disaster. But what I'd forgotten is that Dan is also super receptive to the movements of God, and he will basically do whatever God says, even if it means risking utter financial ruin and a good bit of his personal sanity.

In short, he thought launching a conference was a brilliant idea. He was all in. Even more shocking was that Joe, Jen's husband, who is super prudent and smart about money matters, signed off on this lunacy as well.

I'm still mad at both of them.

A couple of months later, knee-deep in plans and resigned to our fate, I flew to Austin where Jen lives and where we were hosting the first event. We did a walk-through at the hotel we had chosen. We created seating charts, chose lighting, selected menus, and practiced our karaoke dance moves—which, you should know, was an endeavor that confirmed God has a delightful sense of humor.

After we'd finished, Jen and I headed to the hotel restaurant to have lunch. About halfway through our meal, I glanced up and saw the maître d' heading in our direction. When I took a second look and saw who was walking directly behind him, my face contorted in a way that led Jen to ask, "Why are you making such a weird face?"

Thankfully, given my near inability to speak, a response was rendered unnecessary the moment the maître d' pulled out a chair for the table next to us, and Timothy Hutton, the star of *Beautiful Girls*, sat down.

The Timothy Hutton who had popped into our heads when we were contemplating this ridiculous endeavor. The Timothy Hutton whose onscreen rendition of "Sweet Caroline" inspired our theme song. The Timothy Hutton who was so warm and kind and even followed us both back on Twitter! I'm sure he could list a very reasonable explanation for being at that hotel at that moment on that day, and it would even sound plausible. But the truth was God had sent him there to delight us and to confirm for us that this conference-hosting thing, while seemingly insane on the surface, was his ordained insanity. And if you ever want to go on a grand adventure, that's the variety of insanity you want.

(Timothy, my friend, if you are currently pursuing a restraining order against us, and maybe God, too, I get it. No worries.)

I didn't know at that time just how many scary and unexpected directions God was going to lead me in my life. But once again, he was training me to be responsive to his voice. He hung a neon Timothy Hutton–shaped sign in the sky and said, "Yes, Hallie! That's it! You are hearing my voice, and you can trust yourself to know when I am speaking to you, even when the things I say catch you by surprise and scare you a little [or a lot]."

There are so many voices in our lives that try to get our

attention. The voices of those who love us and think they know what's best for us. The voices of those who watch our journey from afar, transpose their own fears and biases onto it, and try to get us to stray from the path we know we're meant to follow. The voices of spiritual attacks that cause self-loathing and doubt. The voices deep within us telling us to learn to trust God but that can also steer us in the wrong direction because of our wounds and insecurities. And then there is the voice of God. The voice that is always kind and encouraging, even when he's correcting us. The voice that always knows what's best for us. The voice that will never betray us. Learning to separate his voice from all the other competing voices takes training. And the Edel Gathering was one piece of my training.

God put the spark of the Edel Gathering into Jen's and my hearts and set it aflame. On paper, none of it made sense. If we were reasonable people, we never would have signed up for it. And by any and all estimations, it should have failed. But it didn't. It didn't because it was God who came up with the crazy idea. He was the One who knocked on our doors and asked if we would like to cooperate with him in bringing it to life. For once, we listened and responded, and through our responding he brought us one step closer to knowing how to follow him into the storms of life.

I don't know much about life and God, but I know this: God does crazy things, loves wild ideas, and is tickled when we sign up to partner with him. This I know. In fact, I am sure of it. So much so that if I had to pick a life motto, it would be this: "If you think God is calling you to do something crazy, he probably is."

ELEVEN

BREATHING TOGETHER

Plenty of people will think you're crazy, no matter what you do. Don't let that stop you from finding the people who think you're incredible—the ones who need to hear your voice, because it reminds them of their own. Your tribe. They're out there.

—Vironika Tugaleva

Two-year-old Sebastian toddled down the aisle of our church, turned left into the row Dan and I, and our eight kids, had monopolized, and quickly crawled into my daughter Sophia's lap. Trailing after him was his sister Maria, who tucked her tiny three-year-old body into the pew between my daughters Lucy and Zelie. Then came Sebastian and Maria's mother, Valerie, ripe and beautiful and pregnant with her tiniest one, due in just three months. I glanced over at all of them and thought, *My people. My tribe. My village.* And I smiled.

I smiled because I had always believed that I was not a person who needed a village. I smiled because I loved them—Valerie and Sebastian and Maria. I smiled because they were and are my people. I smiled because I almost said no to them, not understanding the treasure God was trying to give me. I smiled because God had not taken my no for an answer but instead had quietly tucked my tribe into my heart and into my life. And I loved so much that he had.

I can still vividly remember the first moment I heard Valerie's name, more than five years ago. Dan had come home late at night, after having just finished teaching a class at the church where he worked, to discover his hugely pregnant wife weeping on the couch. He coaxed out of me my tale of woe—stories of tantrums thrown (by me and our children both), drinks spilled, mountains made of laundry, fears fixated on, and bedtimes resisted. He listened, comforted, and then said—because he had no sense of self-preservation, had forgotten who it was exactly he had married, or had decided that desperate times called for desperate measures—"Why don't I ask Valerie and Hannah to come over sometime soon to give you a break? They have offered over and over again, and I know they would be happy to help."

Valerie and Hannah were two young, single, newly out-of-college roommates who went to our church. They were, by all accounts, incredibly sweet and obviously selfless. But I didn't know them, and they didn't know me. Valerie and Hannah, I had heard from Dan, had such beautiful dreams about getting married and having babies and creating homes. But Valerie and Hannah, I knew, would surely watch their dreams die a sudden and horrific death upon walking into my home with its fingerprinted walls, piles of dirty dishes, unmade beds, and children who, though sweet and loving and creative and kind, sometimes questioned whether obedience was something they were interested in embracing. Valerie and Hannah would be horrified by me, who did not seem to be able to get on top of any of the aforementioned issues, no matter how hard I tried.

So I said no. But Dan said yes. And I said no again. This time putting all my strength into winning this tug-of-war. But Dan is stronger than me, and before I knew it, I was face-down in the mud, rope having slipped through my fingers, and he was lifting me back up and telling me to go shower because Valerie and Hannah would be here soon.

Once upon a time, there was a good chance that you would be born into a community of family and friends, and there you would stay—within a maximum of one hundred miles of the place of your birth, if demographic statistics are to be believed—until you breathed your last. Your village was chosen for you, ready-made, eager to embrace and support and guide you.

For a million different and unique reasons, this is no longer true for many, myself included. We move for work, for the military, for financial reasons, or because hard decisions have to be made when we unite ourselves to another, or perhaps God calls us down an unexpected path. Whatever the reason, we often find ourselves planted in a new community, a little wobbly on our feet, and without a tribe who can reach out their hands and steady us. So we have to do the work of searching for our people, which can be very, very scary. Not for everyone, of course. Some people feel comfortable interacting with other human beings, even human beings whom they have never met. Very weird, I know. But for me, and for many, I'm sure, finding my people and making them mine requires an exceedingly intimidating level of vulnerability.

It should not be this way; it would not be this way in a perfect world. But we live in a world where wounded people wound people. So for those of us who might be a little more sensitive or have suffered some painful blows, letting down our shields and opening ourselves up to others is not always an easy thing. Sometimes we don't even know that we're putting a shield between ourselves and others, or that we're hiding in a shell, or that we're only ever peeking out briefly from behind our walls. We smile at people, converse with them as we go about our day, and wish them well, but we can't see that all our interactions are surface level. Our defensive measures are so effective and subtle that we rarely, if ever, let new people deep into our lives.

About five years into motherhood, my friend Nora looked around and saw that she had a bunch of acquaintances but no deep friendships. She saw that she had been so scared of letting people into her mess that she had woven an illusion of perfection around her life—perfect home, perfect marriage, perfect children, perfect Nora. She thought, mistakenly, that if she appeared perfect, no one would ever judge her or want to leave her. But it was all a lie (her words, not mine), because no one ever knew the real Nora. No one knew of her struggles, her pain, her fears, or her failures, and so no one knew she needed support. There was no deep connection with any of her friends, because she hadn't offered them anything to which they could connect.

I have another friend, Sam, who had no problem being honest and open initially. But once she reached a certain level of intimacy with a new friend, she would become afraid and sabotage the relationship. She would stop answering calls or become distant and cold until the other person, wondering what had happened to the friendship that seemed so promising, would quietly walk away.

I understand Sam's fear. Once you allow people access to the most intimate areas of your life, there is a risk that they might begin to see things that you can't see, or maybe that you don't want to see, like harmful habits, deep areas of denial, problematic relationships, your suffering soul. Then they might gently ask you about those things, and you will be forced to acknowledge their existence. And once you see things, you can't unsee them, which compels you to have to deal with them. Sometimes that feels like too high a cost to pay for companionship.

But on the whole, I took another approach. I told myself stories about people. Stories about why they wouldn't like me. Stories about all the terrible characteristics that I, clearly a reader of souls, could intuit they possessed that would lead them to reject me. Stories about why we would be incompatible. Stories that gave me an excuse to not step out of my comfort zone and see whether a person, surely lovely and good in spite of my ridiculous assumptions, might be someone with whom I could connect and share little pieces of my life.

They were never about them, these stories. How could they have been when I didn't know anything about the people who crossed my path for just a moment? The stories were always about me and my fear of rejection. The same was true for Nora and Sam. We feared that people would see all the elements of our lives and turn us away and say we should be ashamed of the mess we had made of everything. We feared that people would confirm our worst fears and harshest judgments about ourselves.

What I know now that I didn't know then is that almost every woman feels this way. Some have just summoned the courage to not let it stand in the way of cultivating friendships.

The thing is, sometimes when you do let people into your mess, they spin around in a circle and, because of their own brokenness, look back at you with something less than perfect charity. Sometimes people can be downright cruel. Most of the time, though, that isn't how it goes. Most of the time people wade into your mess with you and say, "Oh, thank goodness. I thought I was the only train wreck!" But to completely deny that sometimes people will judge you and treat you unkindly would be both a lie and a disservice to ourselves.

The popular advice usually offered is that we should all simply stop caring about what other people think of us. And, yes, that is not a bad thing to do if you can do it. But for some, because of the pain they carry around with them, learning how to stop being affected by the opinions of others will be a lifelong process. That's fine, because I think there is a better approach, anyway.

What we should really be seeking is to become so aware of God's boundless love and affection for us that even if we are rejected and judged, we can still be okay. We can receive that rejection, sit in that hurt, let it wash over us, and then stand up and say, "I am adored and loved and cherished by God to a degree that is unfathomable, so I can handle a little rejection." It doesn't feel so bad, as it turns out. Maybe that's the path we should be choosing. Maybe that is where we will find our courage.

But what if you don't yet know about or feel that insanely wild love God has for you? Well then, your first step is to simply ask him to reveal it to you. And he will. Because he loves you a crazy amount. He does.

Valerie and Hannah stood on one side of the open door, having been summoned by Dan, and I stood on the other, having been forced by Dan. I did that thing I do where I smile big and act all warm and friendly even though on the inside I'm feeling apprehensive and shy, and our first meeting went fine. Better than fine, actually. I immediately fell in love with their sweetness and openheartedness and adorable faces. They were easy to love, these two.

I remember thinking, *Maybe I'm sometimes wrong. Maybe Valerie and Hannah aren't going to walk into my house and be scandalized. Maybe they will see that the house is not chaotic but is teeming with life and love and joy. Or maybe they will see the chaos but feel, as I do, that it is but a small price to pay for all that life and love and joy. Or perhaps they will simply see a very tired pregnant woman and be filled with compassion instead of judgment.*

Whatever their initial reaction, it was the first time

I considered that maybe the stories I told myself were just that—stories, with no basis in reality. And that maybe I needed to more closely examine this tendency of mine to weave these stories into my life. It felt as if God had opened up a little window in my soul, sent in a breeze of insight with a gust of curiosity, and then stepped away, leaving me to ponder it all. I did. And it led me to the realization that all these stories I told were how I protected myself from getting hurt.

This revelation didn't immediately transform me into a person who felt completely at ease when encountering new people and inviting them into my life, but it was the first step. When I catch myself starting to write stories about people, I would stop and examine whether these stories were anything other than complete fiction. If the answer was no, then I would force myself to consider that maybe, just maybe, the person standing before me wasn't going to judge and reject me, that we wouldn't necessarily be incompatible, and perhaps we might even like each other. But even if that were not the case, I would still be all right. I'd survive.

Slowly, over time and with a lot of practice, it became easier to let people in, and my village began to grow—though just a little, as I will always be a person who prefers small tribes over large ones (my unusual gestating tendencies being the obvious exception).

Lest you think that with this epiphany all my village-building issues were resolved, remember that I still had the issue of my introversion to deal with. I had gotten to the point where I could sometimes allow people into my mess, but I was still deeply concerned that once they were there, they might never leave. And, yes, I realize I am a ridiculous person. I do. First I feared people would run in horror from my mess, and then I feared they would never leave. I know. It's a problem. We're working on it, God and I. But this was a real fear that I possessed, and one I knew I needed to conquer, if not for my own sake then for the sake of my children, who were in favor of friends coming over to play and never leaving.

The thing about my introversion is that, unlike my fear of rejection, it was and is never going to go away. It is an essential part of who I am. An extroverted Hallie will never exist in this world. So I had to figure out how to harmonize my new openness to being a part of a village, a community, a tribe, with my God-given temperament. I needed the freedom to explore new potential friendships without fearing them, without worrying that they would somehow take more of me than I had to give. And the answer was simple, as it has proven to be with so many things I've struggled with. Not necessarily easy, but simple. I needed to learn to set and enforce boundaries.

The word *boundary* has always sounded hostile to me. It always felt as if it were implying that I was on one side and a bad person who is out to get me was on the other. And despite all my silly stories about worrying that people will show up and never leave and how the whole thing will be terrible and awkward, in my heart, I've never thought of other people as bad; I've just thought of myself as weird. Because the truth is that we are all a little weird, and part of the work of building friendships is honoring one another's quirks. And to do that, we have to be honest with each other about who we are and what we need.

Just a moment ago, one of my neighbors, a young mom with two young kids, knocked on my door and invited my kids over to play. I wanted to fall at her feet and kiss them and tell her that she was the most beautiful of all the creatures God has ever created. I wanted to start the cause for her canonization and maybe travel to far corners of the world in search of a money tree that I could give to her in gratitude. I had just enough self-control to avoid doing so, mainly because I was afraid she might rescind the invitation, and also because I wasn't 100 percent sure that money trees exist.

What she didn't know was that in issuing that casual invitation, she saved me.

It was Saturday, and I was on a tight deadline. I woke up with plans to write that day. I knew it would be the kind of writing day that involves many interruptions, but since that is how most of my writing gets done, I wasn't worried. But then the interruptions from the kids began, one after another after another. The frequency with which they were volleyed at me was insane. I could not get a single paragraph written without fielding a request or having to answer a question.

I would love to say that I handled this with grace, but I absolutely did not. I would love to say that I saw God moving in the frequent interruptions, gently telling me to adjust my plans and assuring me that he would give me time to write as he saw fit, and that I could rest in knowing that his timing is perfect. But again, that would be a lie. I handled the whole thing with annoyance and a somewhat comical level of incredulity. With each interruption I felt the tension rise within me. My answers got shorter and more irritable, my attitude more ugly, the expressions on my face more ridiculous. It wasn't pretty. And I didn't get a gold star for good behavior.

But then came the knock at the door, the saving grace that I did not deserve and had definitely not earned. I was left with hours of quiet to write in peace. And just like with Valerie and Hannah, I might have missed it if God had not done his work in me, stretching me out of my comfort zone over and over again. I might have missed it had I not learned about boundaries.

So much of the fear I had when it came to letting people into my life was a result of my feeling out of control. And being too much of a people pleaser. It's not a bad thing to want to make people happy, of course, but it can become a bad thing if you are, as I was, so afraid of making people unhappy that you deny and suppress your own needs.

What I didn't understand for a long time is that honoring boundaries isn't about saying no to people but saying yes. Or rather, the nos allow us to issue the greatest yeses there are: Yes, I want you in my life. Yes, let's be in communion. Yes, I will love you.

For so long I felt powerless to express and protect my needs, so I was constantly on the defensive, telling myself, *Don't let anyone get too close, Hallie, because they might violate your personal space, and then what will you do? Well, let them, obviously. Because if you don't, their feelings might get hurt, and it will be entirely your fault.*

A few things about this dysfunctional way of thinking:

1. We are under no obligation to "let" anyone do anything to us. Most people understand this, although it

took me a while. Or maybe I did understand it, but just didn't know how to apply it to my life.

2. When we do share our needs, most people won't have their feelings hurt, even if they don't entirely understand it at first. Honestly, most people will feel honored that you confided in them and were willing to be vulnerable with them. They might think you're a little odd, but that's not such a bad thing, is it?
3. Even if their feelings are hurt, that's not on you. Or me. Or anyone but themselves. As long as we express ourselves with love—and love and firmness are not mutually exclusive—the reactions of others are not our burdens to bear.

My entire life changed once I was able to internalize and act on these truths, because I no longer felt powerless. I could welcome people into my life without fear, knowing that if I needed something in order to remain healthy and whole and at peace, I could simply tell them. And then I could love them.

Last Sunday, as we were driving out of the church parking lot, I spotted a new mom whom I had just met climbing into her car with her husband and baby daughter. I told Dan to stop the car and jumped out like a crazy person. I gestured for her to roll down her window and handed her my contact information in case she ever needed anything, knowing well how hard the early years of motherhood can be. I don't know if she will take me up on my offer, but I felt so much joy in that moment because it was a beautiful illustration of how God had healed me.

Had he not placed his hands on me and, animated by the merest hint of my assent, gently pried open my heart, although I was determined to keep it shuttered closed, I wouldn't have felt comfortable befriending my neighbor or allowing her to sweep my children away and leave me with time to write. I wouldn't have been able to return the favor later that afternoon when her sweet little girl came to play at our house so that her mom could nap. I wouldn't have reached out to that beautiful new mom in the parking lot, inviting her, too, into my life. And that one night when Valerie and Hannah came over might have been the one and only time they did so.

But let me be honest with you. This effort to embrace connection with other human beings has not always gone so smoothly.

A few years back I was traveling home from Kansas, where I had spoken to a beautiful group of women about my many failures, and how God still loves me in spite of them because he's awesome and amazing. I was in the airport about to board my plane when a man came and sat down next to me. I smiled at him, because I was now a person who smiled at people.

He smiled back and began to tell me about the terrible day he was having. I listened and nodded and offered what encouragement I could, and just kept smiling. Everything was going swimmingly, so I thought I'd continue to engage with this man who was having a terrible, no good, very bad day. I said, "Good sir, do you perchance have any grandchildren?"

To which he said, . . . (wait for it) . . . "Do I look like a man who is old enough to have *grandchildren*?"

And then I died.

The end.

You are formally invited to my funeral.

Just kidding. It gets worse. I bet you thought it couldn't get worse.

Instead of quitting while I was ahead, I began rambling about how I have a million children and how I started gestating at a very young age, as did a lot of my friends. In an attempt to convey that I am simply used to encountering younger-than-average grandparents, I made it sound like we were all child brides. It was *super weird*.

He was really mad about it. I felt so bad that I thought about running away, but I was wearing heels and that seemed risky and tiring, and also I was now officially a person who smiled at people so I just kept smiling. Eventually, things kind of, sort of, turned out okay. Maybe. Though I'm pretty sure he's still mad at me.

But you know what? I think God was pretty proud of me. I think he absolutely shook his head and, in an affectionate way, thought, *What am I going to do with this girl?* Because I tried. I tried to be a person who brings love and light into people's worlds, and though sometimes I may also bring weird comments and unintended insults, that doesn't negate the love and light. I did say a little prayer, though, that God would, in his magical God way, remove my comment about grandchildren from this man's brain and only leave the memory of my smiles. (I think smiling was a pretty brilliant idea by me, God, so I hope you were watching.)

Even with this fraught encounter in mind (and let me tell you, I don't think I have to worry about forgetting it anytime soon), when I look back at my transformation, at the work that God has done in teaching me how to better live in communion with people, what strikes me most is that, in the end, it wasn't really that difficult. This huge fear of opening myself up to others I had carried around for so long wasn't that hard to destroy. It just required that I look my fears in the face.

That's the thing about fear: when you don't confront it, you give it power and permission to keep standing behind you, just out of sight, whispering lies into your ear. And those lies can be startlingly compelling. Even the smallest, most insignificant things can cast big shadows. For years I had let these lies convince me that if I looked at strangers in the eye and smiled at them, they would meet my openness with meanness. But then I examined that lie a little, wondered where it came from and when the wound had been inflicted. And because God is amazing, as soon as he saw me questioning the lies, he ran up and met me right there in my curiosity, with answers in hand.

He put his arm around me and reminded me of that time when I was in elementary school at a musical theater class and smiled at a girl standing in front of me at the drinking fountain. I didn't even think about it. I just smiled—which revealed that I hadn't always been afraid of such tiny vulnerabilities. But then she turned back toward me, mouth full of water, and spit all over me, leaving me mortified and ashamed and confused because I'd never met this girl. Why would someone do that? What was it about me that offended and enraged her so?

As this incident replayed in my mind, I realized, that was

when and how the lie that strangers were always one second away from hurting me and that my only hope of emerging unscathed was to make myself invisible began.

The lie told me that everyone was secretly like this. That if I continued to open myself up to others, even in small ways, they would continue to do the equivalent of turning and spitting on me. And the little girl who still lives inside me—or at least comes to visit sometimes—was terrified of that possibility. She was terrified of feeling mortified and rejected and unloved again. She was terrified that when faced with the pain of rejection, she still wouldn't know how to react to it. Therefore she built up a wall so that no one could ever hurt her like that again.

The truth, though, is that, yes, some people are hurting so badly that they lash out at others in cruel ways in an attempt to release some of their pain. Or maybe so that they won't feel so alone, having been hurt themselves. Or possibly to protect themselves from further abuse. But most people don't do this. Most people are good and kind and loving.

It was Father Manno, who is never afraid to challenge me, knowing both my fears and my desire to be free of them, who suggested I start smiling at people in the grocery store. He told me to lift my eyes up from the ground and simply encounter people. To see them and let them see me, and then just see what happens.

So I did.

And I discovered that I love people. I love meeting them and making them smile. I love hearing their stories and laughing with them and talking about the best brands and flavors of ice cream (Blue Bell mint chocolate chip, if you're curious). I love being in communion with them. I do.

I know. I am as surprised by this turn of events as anyone.

In the end, all I needed was one small nudge. All I needed was for someone to encourage me to turn and look my fear in the face and see for myself that it was a liar. To see that, yes, sometimes people are unkind, but most of the time they are delightful. To see that I was no longer that little girl who was new in class and didn't know how to handle cruelty. That I was, instead, a woman who would feel my heart surge with love when I encountered people who were struggling. A woman who would recognize the sadness inside them, and, instead of being afraid of it, would desire to heal and soothe it and to make them feel loved.

That was the truth that was obscured for so long. I just couldn't see it until I faced the lie that sought to conceal it.

Hannah now lives a few hours away with her husband, son, and their newest little one, a girl named Evie. Hannah remains an integral part of our family, and we love her so much. Valerie moved away for a while but is back now, and it fills me with such happiness to have her back with me. The two of them came into my life during one of my most difficult seasons and poured so much mercy and kindness that it still takes my breath away. They fed us and cleaned for us and loved on our kids. They gave me space to breathe and time to sleep and kept me sane. They became my sisters. That was more than five years ago, and so much has changed since then.

I am now in a new season of life, one that is much less stressful and involves significantly more sleep. And my Valerie is the one who is woken up at night, and she has no older kids to help her with the younger ones. She has an extraordinary husband who heroically serves our country, who is currently deployed while she is in her third trimester. He will be deployed, in fact, for the entirety of her third trimester. So this time I get to love on her, and it's one of my greatest joys and honors.

I get to watch Sebastian and Maria while she runs errands or goes to the doctor or simply takes some time to catch her breath. I get to welcome her into my home and insist that she put her feet up while my girls play with her kids. I get to invite her to church so that she can soak up God's love while we pass her sweet babes from lap to lap to lap. I get to feed her and listen to her and tell her that it is all going to be okay. And I hope she knows it's true, because she's seen me at my worst and emerge from my worst.

This is what being a part of a village means. It means breathing together and being vulnerable with one another and lifting one another out of the darkness and into the light. It means drinking margaritas and laughing and commiserating and being unafraid to reveal the parts of yourself that make you feel ashamed and embarrassed. It means offering help and accepting help even when you feel like a burden. It means being honest about what you need. It means allowing God to bond you together so closely that it begins to feel unnatural when you have gone too long without doing any of these things.

And it means letting your people reveal things about yourself that you didn't know. Like maybe you were never quite as much of an introvert as you thought. Maybe you were just a little scared.

TWELVE

TASTING SWEETNESS

Almost everything will work again if you unplug it for a few minutes, including you.

—Anne Lamott

Some women covet other women's abilities to create beautiful, welcoming, perfectly decorated homes. Some of us wish we were Nigella, the food writer who God apparently saw fit to give insane cooking skills and also crazy beautiful looks, which, if he's asking, doesn't really seem fair. Others—and, no, I'm not thinking of anyone in particular—are wildly jealous of green-thumbed women who have gardens that love them and give them beautiful, fragrant bouquets, one after another, with which they can fill their homes.

I once had a friend who was literally a rocket scientist, and though I have no particular interest in rockets or science, I have felt a few pangs of envy that she had been given a brain so vastly superior to mine. Oh, and women who have been filled to bursting with artistic talent? They are a little like unicorns to me. I have no hope of ever becoming one, but I'm fascinated by them and drawn to them and secretly hope that if I can tiptoe slowly and get up close enough, a little of their magic might rub off on me.

I'm still waiting, sadly.

I can live with these things, though. I can make peace with my insufficiencies and celebrate others' gifts. At the end of the day, despite mild pangs of envy, I am just so delighted that God created all these beautiful people and gave them so many uniquely extraordinary gifts, which they are now using to saturate our world with color and life and goodness. It's delightful.

There is this one thing, though. One little gift that I wish I possessed but don't. One tiny talent that I've chased after but thus far have been unable to catch. One small endeavor that I've tried and failed repeatedly to achieve for over thirty years. It is ridiculous and silly and inexplicable that I haven't been able to let it go and move on with my life, but I haven't.

I want to be a person who journals.

I want to have a row of well-worn notebooks of different colors and sizes lined up on my bookshelf. I want to be able to flip through those notebooks and remind myself of the exact date that certain things happened and how I felt about them at the time. I want for there to be mementos and photographs taped to the pages and possibly even colorful illustrations in the margins—created by me, naturally, because in this fantasy I possess at least a modicum of artistic talent. I want the pages to be filled with funny stories and inspiring quotes and perhaps even an odd recipe or two.

I don't know why I can't let this go. Why I can't look back at my long history of being unable to commit to journaling and make peace with the fact that this is not a hobby that is meant to be mine. Why I can't just accept that when God threw in all the ingredients that were to make up the person I was to become, he didn't throw in a pinch of journaling acumen.

I should probably let this go and move on with my life. But my daughter Zelie just received a Barnes & Noble gift card, and while she's redeeming it, I have every intention of buying yet another beautiful, blank Moleskine journal. I even know exactly what I will use that journal for. It's a foolproof plan, really, which is good considering it took me over three decades to come up with it.

I am going to start a gratitude journal. Just a sentence or two or three a day. Minimal commitment and lots of inspiration from which to draw. On the first page I will write: "If you want to know what God's love feels like, ______________." I will then fill in the blank once a day. I even have the first few entries all planned out.

I will start with, "Get yourself a hug from Cardinal Dolan," which, by the way, he is known to give out to anyone and everyone who crosses his path. So get yourself down to St. Patrick's Cathedral in New York City, stat. I managed to get one when I was in the city earlier this month, and I'm still smiling. He is one of the sweetest people I have ever met. Truly a teddy bear of a man. And his hugs are out of this world.

I will then follow that up with, "Sniff as many newborn necks as you can," and "Eat warm, fresh fruit pie every single day of the summer season." I might also add a "note to self" about how Blue Bell ice cream is the best ice cream with which to top warm pies, in case I somehow forget that in my old age. I can't see that happening, but one never knows.

"Take long bubble baths in the evening, and even longer walks on the beach at sunset," "Always play music when you're cleaning or cooking dinner," "Gather as many kisses as you can," and "Give birth to a tribe of cute girls who rub your feet when you're pregnant and call you 'pretty mama' "—all would make the list.

Oh, and "Spend irresponsible amounts of money at posh salons on a regular basis" would most definitely have a spot of honor somewhere on page one. You may be asking, "Is that really what God's love feels like, Hallie? Are you sure?" And to that I say yes. Absolutely it is. And not just because of the aromatherapy in the air or the sound of water flowing through the mini-fountains or the scalp massages (if you don't currently frequent a salon that massages your scalp, we should talk), but because sometimes in life you lose sight of yourself a bit, and a good hairstylist can help you find it.

I mean that sincerely.

There was a moment years ago, during a season of painful struggle and overwhelming challenges, when I looked at myself in the mirror and thought, *I don't recognize the person looking back at me. This is not who I am. This is not who I see when I close my eyes and imagine myself. And this is certainly not who I want to be.*

The person I wanted to be, the person I saw when I closed my eyes, was a woman who loved dressing up for date nights in vintage dresses and bright lipstick. A woman who derived an odd amount of joy from using hot rollers on her hair and then saturating it with hair spray, because "the higher the hair, the closer to God." (I am pretty sure this is an absolute truth that has been affirmed by the Vatican.) And a woman who loves Sephora with an everlasting and unshakeable love that is a little out of control.

But the woman I saw in the mirror that day hadn't set foot in a salon in over a year. Her makeup collection felt a distinct lack of love and affection. Her favorite dresses were wondering what had gone so terribly wrong in their lives that they had lost the battle against yoga pants and hoodies. And though I can joke about it in retrospect, the woman I saw was deeply sad.

Self-care as a concept gets a lot of hate. Perhaps it's because it shares four letters with the word *selfish*. For whatever reason, saying, or even thinking, that you want and need to make self-care a priority in your life feels like a revolutionary decision. One that feels safer whispered than boldly stated. One that implies, especially in the darker and more desperate moments, that perhaps you don't love your family (or God) quite enough, because if you did, you would dig down deep and summon the motivation to do whatever needs to be done for them, regardless of the cost. I tried that approach for a few years, by the way, which is how I ended up burned out and knowing far more about Kanye and the Kardashians than anyone probably should, and I say that with a good bit of affection for them all.

A while back, when I was trying to figure out how to pull myself out of my Season of Sadness, I talked about it with my friend Belen. She said,

> What helped me, Hallie, was to stop thinking of it as self-care and start thinking of it as resourcing. Every day I wake up with a to-do list that feels endless, but it's a to-do list that I love because it's full of work that God has given me and tasks oriented toward caring for people I love. I want to be able to continue to do this work, and, if possible, I'd like to be able to do it without feeling miserable, which isn't likely unless I first acquire the resources I need to fuel me. For me that's ballet class, time for prayer, McDonald's french fries, and a monthly Margarita Night with my friends. If I don't get these things, I burn out really quickly. It's as simple as that. If you really want to pull yourself out of this rut, you have to figure out where you are going to get your fuel from.

She went on to tell me a story about how, seven years into motherhood, she found herself uncontrollably weeping on the kitchen floor because the heart-shaped brownies she was trying to make for her son to discover upon returning home from school looked less like hearts and more like the contents of his little sister's diaper. At that moment, she had an epiphany of sorts. She knew she should be laughing, but all she could do was cry, and it occurred to her that there might be a problem.

Later that night, she sat down with her husband and poured her heart out to him. She told him how tired she was and how everything made her cry and about the despair that seemed to follow her around day after day. She wasn't depressed, she didn't think. She just felt uninspired and empty and a little hopeless.

He loved on her and listened, having learned years ago that problem solving should come only after adequate catharsis and that trying to rush to the solution stage would only bring very bad things into his life. Finally, after he intuited that it was safe to make a small suggestion or two, he mentioned he had noticed she hadn't been sleeping much. He told her,

> You go to work early in the morning so that you can be home for the kids in the afternoon, and then you stay up later than the rest of us, washing the clothes and ironing them. Does it really matter if the kids' clothes are ironed? Also, maybe they don't need fresh-baked snacks every single day after school. And don't kill me, honey, because I love you and you are my queen and I see that scary look starting to cross your face, but those enrichment activities they do every day after school? I feel like maybe some of those could go too. Just give them a pile of dirt. Same with the crafts. And as long as I'm risking my life here, I need you to know that I might die if I ever see glitter again. Why don't we choose sleep over glitter, honey? You and me together. Let's make that brave decision.

And then he got into the duck-and-cover position.

Belen admitted that it was hard to hear him because her first instinct was to interpret his words as a lack of appreciation for all the sacrifices she had been making for her family. After stewing for a bit, though, she realized what her husband was trying to say was that he loved her so much that if all those things disappeared tomorrow but left a smile on her face, it would be far better than if she continued to slave away until all the joy had left her heart.

After hearing Belen's story, I thought about the things that had fueled me in the past, and I realized that, more than anything, I missed my salon. I really, really missed it. And I sensed that it wasn't just vanity tugging at my heartstrings. There was something deeper that I was yearning for. So temporarily ignoring my budget, I went to the salon, and it was everything I knew it would be. It was bliss. They pampered me and made me feel human again. The scents and sounds that floated through the air relaxed me in a way that I had forgotten I could be relaxed. You know that question, "Would you choose to have a cook, a housekeeper, a nanny, or a chauffeur?" I would choose "None of the Above" and write in: "Scalp Massage Therapist." I don't even know if such a glorious variety of specialist exists, but that would be my choice.

As I exited the salon, I caught sight of my reflection in the salon window. Though momentarily distracted by the *Singin' in the Rain*–era Debbie Reynolds-esque bounciness of my hair and tempted to rush back inside and threaten my stylist until she revealed all her secrets to me, it wasn't my hair that ultimately captured my attention. It was the fact that I was standing a little taller and walking with a bit more spring in my step. For the first time in a long time, I saw hope in my eyes.

Some might call me shallow or accuse me of vanity, but a woman who feels beautiful is a woman who will go forth and set the world on fire. Different things make different women feel beautiful. For some, a rich book that allows her to get lost in another world and leaves her imagination running wild will make her feel beautiful. For others, exercise that leaves her cheeks pink and her lungs full will do the trick. For others still, creating art that leaves her nose smudged with paint will make her feel like the loveliest creature on earth. For me, it's all those things to some degree, but if I need a quick and effective pick-me-up, I will find it at the salon every time.

I went home and looked at the challenges that were staring back at me. There were many. Two hours prior I was so overwhelmed by them that I had almost cancelled my haircut appointment. But now I was not only undaunted but excited and energized by the work laid out before me. I looked around and thought, *Well, the good news is that Hallie is back. So get excited, everyone, because this is my home and these are my loves. And though the problems I face today are many, I am not going down without a fight.*

Basically, I was General Patton, but with better hair.

It has been said that the mother is the heart of the home. And when that heart ceases to beat with abandon, to be strong and animated, to love with unrestrained passion, things get pretty bad pretty quickly. I knew in that moment that I never wanted to be back in the place I had been standing just minutes before entering the salon, and for years prior to that. While I was still riding the high of an amazing haircut, I wanted to do the work of figuring out what resources I needed to seek out on a daily basis to be the thriving heart of the home I yearned to be.

Being an introvert, I knew I needed to prioritize quiet time over sleep—though sleep was still important—so kids' bedtimes would need to be locked down. I needed to be able to exercise each day, so Dan and I made a plan that I would head out every evening after dinner while he held down the fort. I needed time each day to talk to Jen on the phone, which meant casting off the mom guilt that told me my full attention should be on my children whenever they were remotely within my orbit. I needed to seek out the things that set me on fire and energized me, so I added regular bubble baths, reading good books, savoring mint chocolate chip ice cream, and time to chat with God to the list of nonnegotiables.

I also needed to understand that caring for myself might look different from what I had envisioned.

When I was pregnant with my eighth child and on the cusp of my third trimester, I flew to Indiana to speak to a beautiful group of women about self-care, of all things. The flight over was smooth, the hotel room peaceful and quiet, and the event a joy. The women and I talked about what caring for yourself looks like in different seasons, how we can carve out time for restoring our souls and bodies, and why self-care is not a bad thing but rather a God-given duty.

When you think and speak about a subject so often, it's easy to assume, mistakenly, that you have a pretty firm grasp on the topic. You probably don't know everything, of course, but you sense there aren't any huge surprises left to discover.

Silly me. How could I have forgotten that one of the best things about God is that he never stops surprising us and presenting us with opportunities to surprise ourselves?

There aren't too many flights out of Evansville, Indiana, so when I booked my trip, I chose a flight that left in the afternoon on Sunday. Because what kind of a crazy person would take a flight that left at six in the morning while pregnant and on the cusp of her third trimester?

After the event ended on Saturday, I stopped by Fresh Market and stocked up on delicious things to eat, requested late checkout from the hotel, put on my pajamas, climbed into bed, turned on HGTV, and prepared to enjoy a quiet evening. But instead, I started to cry. And cry. And then I cried some more. Right into my delicious mini cheesecake.

At first I felt really, really guilty. What kind of pregnant mom of eight receives the gift of almost twenty-four hours of peace and quiet in a hotel room and then cries about it? What kind of ungrateful person does that when her husband is at home watching the kids by himself so she can have this break? But cry I did. Why? Because in that moment I wanted nothing more in the entire world than to be back home with my family.

I tried hard to force myself to savor the evening. I really did. But I just couldn't get there. So I sent Dan a text message telling him that I wanted to come home and was thinking of trying to switch my flight to one at six in the morning. To this, knowing how I feel about early mornings, he wisely replied, "Whoa . . . that sounds extremely painful for you."

He wasn't wrong. *Extremely* might have even been an understatement. But still, I wanted to try, although I didn't think it would be possible. We didn't have room in the budget for a huge change fee and rate adjustment, and I have never, in all my years of travel, tried to change a flight without incurring additional cost. In fact, it was stated clearly on the website and on my ticket that changing my flight would cost no less than two hundred dollars, which we didn't have to spare.

But I blew my nose and said a prayer and called the airline anyway. The kind customer agent who took my call clicked a few keys, put me on hold, and said, "There will be no cost associated with this change. Would you like me to find you a seat on the six o'clock flight?"

I replied by crying loudly and thanking him effusively over and over and over again. I might have even promised to name my child after him. I can't be sure. I gratefully accepted my little miracle, said goodbye to my night of binge-watching "reality" television, put down the snacks I bought, set my alarm for 3:45 a.m., and went to sleep. The next morning, I drove to the airport before the sun rose and flew home.

I was exhausted and nauseous and shaky . . . and had not a single regret.

I love hotel rooms. I love snacks. I love late checkouts and sleeping in. If you had asked me a week prior, I would have told you that all those are the first things I think of when I think of self-care. But that weekend, self-care looked like coming home to my family. It looked like getting up early instead of sleeping in. It looked like eating a stale breakfast at the airport instead of a fresh one at the hotel. It looked like being exhausted instead of well rested. It looked like cooking dinner and tucking little ones into bed instead of reading quietly on a plane.

It looked like everything my heart needed in that moment.

When you practice self-care—and I hope you do and will—leave room for surprises. Leave room for what needs to look nothing like what you thought you wanted. And leave room for God to whisper, *Put down that cheesecake, say goodbye to Joanna Gaines, and come with me. I have a flight waiting for you.*

I think sometimes we get stuck in the mentality that because the work we do is important—whether in our careers, in communities, or at home—we couldn't possibly take a break. All we can see are the things that are not getting accomplished when we rest and pause. And because of this longing to do good in the world, we are often blind to the fact that even less will get done if we don't keep our batteries charged and our hearts protected and whole.

Avoiding death, or burning out if you want to be less melodramatic about the whole thing, is an excellent reason to prioritize self-care or resourcing or whatever you feel comfortable calling it. But there's an even more important reason, and it is simply this: God loves you and wants only good things for you. I know sometimes it doesn't feel that way, but it's true.

This is not to say that God will not lead us through seasons of suffering or ask us to endure painful things or refine us by fire. Because he absolutely will. But even during those trials—especially during those trials—he wants to tenderly grasp our hands and kiss away our tears and love us through every moment.

He wants us to taste sweetness even when we are being asked to drink from a cup of bitterness. He wants to give us rest even when we are being woken up twelve times a night by a baby who will be soothed only by the warmth of our breasts and the comfort of our arms. He wants us to seek out and embrace joy even amid the most excruciating pain and suffering. He wants us to be fierce even when we would much rather hide under the safety of our blankets.

He wants all of these simply because he loves us.

Think for a moment about a young woman in your life whom you love dearly. Now imagine her carrying a heavy cross, physical or spiritual in nature, but refusing help and rejecting rest. Consider how you would feel if she never treated herself with kindness or allowed herself to savor the simple, delicious pleasures of life. Imagine if she felt that she had to earn your love, or worse, she felt she was unworthy of it entirely. That would break your heart.

But that is exactly what we do. We withhold that same mercy, love, and compassion from ourselves all the time. And where does that leave us? Exhausted, angry, resentful, and completely unprepared to fight the battles we must fight to become the women we are meant to become and live the lives we are meant to live.

You are a warrior. Even on the days that you don't feel like one. And sometimes even warriors need a good salon.

THIRTEEN

INDWELLING

Christ asks for a home in your soul, where he can be at rest with you, where he can talk easily to you, where you and he, alone together, can laugh and be silent and be delighted with one another.

—Caryll Houselander

I have given birth in my car and in my bedroom and twice in my bathroom. I have delivered new life in a birth cottage and three times in a hospital; or four, if you count the time our tiny Clementine was taken from my body while I lay unconscious and hemorrhaging in the operating room.

Each experience I have had of pregnancy and birth has been different. I have experienced the heights of euphoria and the depths of pain, despair, and anxiety. But every time, I have emerged from pregnancy having learned something new about myself and the nature of God. Never once have I walked away without being transformed. Every single time I gazed down upon the tiny newborn nestled in my arms, I have been thunderstruck by the thought, *I may have been the one to give birth to you, but you have made me new.*

Even Clementine. I may never have had the chance to hold her, but by bringing me into the depths of grief, she revealed the limitlessness of God's mercy. And no one ever walks away from an encounter with such grief or mercy unchanged.

My pregnancy with my oldest son, Daniel, was fairly textbook. The morning sickness was not my favorite, nor was the sciatica pain. But all in all it was a healthy, enjoyable experience, full of eager anticipation that is reserved solely for first-time parents. There was a moment, though, during the transition phase of labor, when I felt a level of pain that I had never experienced before and have not experienced since. I felt certain that my bones were going to shatter. Even as I type about this now, removed from the moment by fourteen years, it doesn't feel melodramatic.

I remember looking into my mother's eyes and saying, "I cannot do this." And I truly believed I could not.

She in turn looked into my eyes, in that somehow simultaneously fierce and gentle way that only mothers can, and assured me, "Yes, you can. You are. And you will."

In that moment, I had the most profound experience of my strength waning to nothing and God's power surging within me. That's what he does. He comes to us when we are broken and bleeding and utterly depleted and takes over. We may not feel his presence as intensely as I did then. But almost all of us can look back at a time in our life and say, "I have no idea how I survived that." And that's how we know he was there, with us, loving us, breathing life into us when we otherwise would have expired.

My second child, Jack, gifted me with a birth experience that was so painless the doctor kept asking, as he looked at the contraction monitor and saw each new wave rock my body, "Are you sure you can't feel that? Or that? Nothing? Nothing at all?" At one point, he looked at the nurse and asked, "Are you sure she didn't get an epidural?" The labor was that easy.

The pregnancy itself, though, was full of anxiety and fear. Not fear of anything that was happening to me but of what might one day come to pass. I feared the future and the amorphous shadows that haunted my imagination. Through those nine months, God began to teach me about the importance of staying grounded in the present moment, and accepting all the peace and joy and grace that he so wants to give me in any given moment.

So, of course, he capped it off with a painless labor, after I had spent months fretting over whether I had the strength to endure it, coming as Jack did, just eleven months after Daniel. It was a reminder that I shouldn't waste my time agonizing over things that have not yet come to pass—and may never come to pass.

My Sophia was born in the car. Of course she was. She is the most social of all my social-butterfly children. I can only imagine how waiting the extra ten minutes to get to the hospital would have been too much for her already extroverted infant heart to bear. She slipped into the world in darkness on the side of a residential street.

The season in which I carried her within me was one of profoundly low self-esteem. I was overcome with feelings of being unworthy and unlovable and deeply unattractive. But when I gave birth to Sophia in the car, on the side of that road, I felt like Wonder Woman or maybe Joan of Arc. Her birth, too, healed something in me that desperately needed healing.

I was pregnant with my Lucy when we were in Texas, during a season in which Dan and I felt so estranged. When I look back on the pregnancy, nothing sticks out at me. It was normal, and my midwife was incredible. Having done this three times before, I felt like I knew what I was doing. But I was sad, too, because Dan felt so distant. It seemed as if no matter how hard I swam in his direction, the tide of our alienation kept sweeping me farther away from him. But then, during labor, he held my hand and encouraged me and wiped my brow with cold cloths. Now, when I look back on that night, I feel encouraged, because I know that no matter what happens, Dan and I will always be an awesome parenting team.

When I was thirty-six weeks pregnant with Zelie, Dan was laid off from his job as the assistant programming manager at the local Catholic radio station; a result of the Deepwater Horizon oil spill, which devastated the economy along the Gulf Coast. All the things I had been struggling with inside me came to a head. Just when I was beginning to feel like we could see a light at the end of the tunnel that was our marital and financial struggles, we were plunged back into darkness. When I look back on the last month of my pregnancy, I see my rock-bottom moment. The moment that I looked up at God and said, "No, I'm serious this time. I have nothing left to give. I'm out."

But then, because he is brilliant and knows my heart and my needs with a level of intimacy that is breathtaking, he gave me Zelie. And, as only fresh-from-the-womb babies can do, she gave me hope. Life was still hard, and I was still mired in darkness, but she was the force that made me think that maybe I had a little tiny bit left to give. That maybe I could stand back up one more time and continue walking.

My pregnancy with Charlie revealed to me that pregnancy in your midthirties looks nothing like pregnancy in your twenties. By which I mean, it is exponentially more difficult and miserable. At least that has been my experience. I have a friend who said she prefers her later-in-life pregnancies over her earlier ones, because she knows better how to care and advocate for herself. This is absolutely true. But still, the difficulty and the misery that comes with it are not insignificant.

The beautiful thing about this pregnancy, though, was that God brought Valerie and Hannah into my life, who supported and encouraged and lifted me up with their selfless sweetness. I exited that pregnancy with a heart so much more receptive to God expressing his love through others.

And then Max came along. My Max, whose due date just happened to fall on the first day of a weekend-long conference I was hosting for 350 women. Max, who decided to be born two weeks after his so-called due date. Max, who held his head at such an angle that I experienced those same two weeks as endless days and nights of prodromal labor.

Max, who decided to be born so suddenly that I was left to deliver him, sunny-side up, all by myself in my bathroom. Max, who, as soon as I held him in my arms, made me ready to do it all again. My love for him gave me such insight into the depths of God's love for us.

And, of course, my Clementine, who taught me that there is no darkness that cannot be scattered by the light of God's love. That's a pretty amazing feat for a girl who was tucked within my body for a mere eleven weeks.

Last, but certainly not least, sweet Penelope. My rainbow baby. Her little life, as new as it is, has been a testament to the fact that night is always followed by day, darkness by light. My pregnancy with her was the hardest, physically and mentally speaking, that I have ever experienced. I was in pain from start to finish, threw up for all nine months, and was overwhelmed with such intense pregnancy-induced anxiety that I spent many three-in-the-morning hours planning fire escape routes. I came under a level of spiritual attack that I had never before experienced. But then, just weeks after she was born, God met and lifted that darkness in the blink of an eye and, in the most unexpectedly beautiful way, poured so much of his grace and healing power into me that I emerged a new and different person.

What strikes me as I look back at my pregnancies is that, over and over again, by welcoming babies into my womb, I welcomed suffering into my life. Not something I am known to do.

I heard once that everyone has one root sin out of three: pride, vanity, or sensuality. We all, of course, struggle to some degree with all three. But for most of us, one of these three will trip us up and exert more of a negative influence over our life.

1. *Pride*, as I understand it, is a disordered attachment to our own excellence;
2. *vanity*, to the approval of others; and
3. *sensuality*, to comfort, ease, and pleasure.

For me there is no distant second. It's all sensuality all the time in Hallie land. Almost every vice that I have mightily struggled against has been rooted in my desire for comfort, ease, and pleasure. This is probably why God peeked down from heaven, grabbed his notepad and pencil, and scribbled: "Send Hallie eight children. Minimum. Otherwise she's doomed."

As one might guess, having eight children doesn't leave as much time as one might hope for comfort and ease, though they do bring an extraordinary amount of pleasure.

So send them God did. But he couldn't have without my consent. I had to open myself up and accept all these new little lives and the suffering that came with them. But in a turn of events that shocks no one more than me, I did consent and open and accept. When I wonder why I did, the answer is always the same: love.

Just that. Love.

Over and over again, though I moaned and complained and wailed from beginning to end of every pregnancy, each time I beheld the sight of my newest child for the first time, I thought, *Well, aren't you a delicious baby? Once again, it was all worth it. Without a doubt. Every last ache and anxious thought. All the sacrifices and the many little deaths I had to embrace. And I would do it all again.*

God is endlessly creative, and he has a million ways to heal a soul. With me, he wanted to heal my soul by having me make of myself a dwelling place. A dwelling place into which he could pour so much love that I couldn't help but be healed. Because that's what love does. It heals. That is love's nature, and its most ardent desire. Love is God. And God is Love. And both, being one and the same, yearn to enter into our beings and make us whole and healthy and so extraordinarily happy.

So God made of me a dwelling place. And through all those seasons, and with such love and intimacy, he revealed areas of myself that were sick in some way. Shame that needed to be brought out into the light and purified. Hidden, diseased parts of me into which he needed to pour his purifying love. Weaknesses he needed to strengthen. Fears he needed to destroy. Wounds he needed to heal.

As one baby after another dwelled within me and filled me full to bursting with love, as I began to heal, I thought about the fact that God, too, dwells within me. This truth is so huge, a mystery nearly unfathomable, that, even having gestated nine times, I am still grasping to wrap my mind around it.

This is what I know: God finds us so captivating that he will never stop pursuing us. God sees such beauty in each one of us that he wants to make of us a sacred space in which to dwell. God desires to live within that sacred space with us forever in divine unity. And through this pursuit and indwelling, God means to make us into new creatures more full of light and love and fire than we ever could have conceived.

But I also know this: God did not make us to be slaves or fashion us to be robots. God created us to be his children. People of free will. Individuals who, when called, have a decision to make. Will we follow? Will we say yes? Will we be receptive and open? Will we beg him to enter into us and make of us his dwelling place? Or will we turn away?

At every moment of each day this is a decision we must make.

I know. Do we not have enough on our plates with all the laundry and jobs and meal planning and errand running and volunteering and loving on husbands and deep conditioning of our hair and chick-lit reading and snuggling with kids and the rest? Now we have to make big indwelling decisions all day too?

Yes and no. For the most part, I think God just wants to hang out with us. He wants to stand next to us while we do our laundry and listen to us tell him how sometimes the task feels endless but also brings us such joy knowing that he saw fit to give us people we can love and serve. He wants to ride along in our cars and occasionally remind us that the person who just cut us off might just be distracted by some challenge or tragedy rather than being, at the core, a terrible and unredeemable person. He wants to hold us when we cry because the thing we just said to our spouse that was meant to uplift got all twisted in the delivery and now our spouse is mad and hurt and we miss them. He wants to sit with us while we binge-watch our favorite show and delight in our delight.

Allow him to do that. Welcome him into all the moments of your day—that is, ask him to dwell within you. It really is as simple as that.

Years ago I had an experience I will never forget. I was praying one morning at a beautiful church in Austin, Texas. I don't remember what brought me there at that particular time of day, but I do remember that I was the only person present and that it was perfectly still and quiet and cool inside. The sun shone through the stained glass and highlighted the dancing dust in its rays, which is one of my favorite things to see. It was peaceful and beautiful, but I was restless and angry.

I was angry that Dan and I were struggling so much. Angry at God for not easing our financial burdens. Angry that I didn't know how to fix things. And angry that God had not, at least as far as I could perceive, offered me much consolation amid all these trials. I felt utterly abandoned by God and all my hurt and frustration and anger came pouring out of me in prayer—that is, if you consider angry words directed at God to be a sort of prayer, which I do.

In fact, I think such words are some of God's favorite prayers, because when we go to him and lay ourselves bare, holding back nothing and exposing everything, well, that's when we are finally being honest with God. And he can take it. He already knows all that is in our hearts anyway.

Some of my most ridiculous moments have been when I've gone to God and tried to convince him that I was more detached from something than I was. Or more at peace. Or more forgiving or understanding. He knew I wasn't any of those things—I am not generally—and wanted me to come to him and let him into my struggle and suffering so he could soothe and comfort and heal me.

It hadn't proven terribly effective, historically speaking, when he had come to me and asked, "Hey, Hallie. What do you say I rub a little salve into that gash on your heart?"

Because my response had often been, "What gash? There's no gash here. I'm fine. Just *fine*," and then run away.

He will pursue us, but he will never trap us. He loves us, but we have to be open to receiving that love to know it. He will heal us, but only after we give him access to our wounds.

On that day in the church I wasn't running away. No, on that day, I had run toward God and was pummeling him with all my might.

And then he hugged me.

That was exactly what it felt like and, at the same time, comes nowhere close to adequately describing it. I felt overwhelmed and possessed by love in a way I never had before. It felt just like that hug Cardinal Dolan gave me but times a million. It was ecstasy and euphoria and brought me the most immense sense of relief because life was hard. But life during this difficult season without the consolation of God had been agony. When God overtook me with his love, life was still hard, but the agony was lifted.

That was more than ten years ago, and I have been chasing after that feeling ever since. I want to find it again, to experience its singular high once more, but I'm not surprised that it remains elusive. God wanted it to mean something, for me to remember it, and for it not to become a daily grace that I might be tempted to take for granted. There was more that he wanted to teach me about indwelling.

He wanted me to take that experience of being overtaken by his love and know that it was the goal of the spiritual life. He wanted me to live in a perpetual state of being utterly intoxicated by him. To allow him to dwell so fully within me that I felt pregnant with his love. In the church that day, he gave me the hunger for it, and I was left with an intense desire to satisfy it.

It's funny how often we overcomplicate things in the spiritual life. I wanted God to dwell more fully within me, and I assumed at first that figuring out how to make that happen required diving into deep philosophical waters and undertaking complicated practices. But God wants to come and make a home within all of us. Even those of us who sometimes feel like we're drowning when we try to swim in those deep waters, or who are going to have to wait a couple of decades (at least) until our lives contain room for long and involved spiritual exercises. He wants to overwhelm all of us with his love, and so he makes it very, very simple. "Just be receptive," he says. "Open yourself up to me. Remove the barriers. Invite me in."

Simple in concept, anyway. But not always so simple in execution. To let God dwell within us is to make ourselves naked and vulnerable, and that can be a scary thing. So we start putting up walls. If we take an honest look at ourselves and our lives—if we spin in a circle a time or two and really gaze at the walls we have erected around ourselves—we often find that we have done some pretty impressive construction work.

I knew I was doing it, and I knew I had to stop doing it if I wanted to taste again that bliss I had experienced in the church that day. I knew I needed to tear down all those bricks of vice and apathy and distraction, one by one, and let God in. Because he wasn't going to force his way in; he's going to wait for my invitation.

Maybe at first we can only remove one brick. That's okay. God is patient. He will shine as much light as he possibly can through that little opening. And the great thing about God's light is that it is so awesome that even a tiny bit of it will give you the strength to take down a second brick, and then a third, until that wall of yours begins to crumble. When that happens, which admittedly can be a rather long process—I'm still discerning which of my bricks would be the least painful to part with next—the love party starts, bringing with it all the euphoria and ecstasy and bliss that I experienced over ten years ago in the church.

The more we open ourselves up to God, the more barriers we remove, the more fervent the invitation we issue, the more constant our attempts to stay in his presence and bring him into every moment of our day, the more he will be able to come and dwell within us.

And when you have God dwelling within you, you will have the strength to be your fiercest self. To dive into the cosmos of the unknown and fall home into a life of incandescence.

CONCLUSION

RISE

I attempted to jump on our eight-foot trampoline last week. I had forgotten how terrifying it can be to jump on a trampoline. My children had hidden this fact from me with a troublingly impressive level of deception, so I had not realized that to step foot on a trampoline at my age is basically equivalent to saying to the universe, "You have had your fun with me, and I with you, and it has been lovely." Dust to dust by way of ill-advised acrobatic decision.

But not before I had one last epiphany . . .

Less than five years ago, I was talking to Jen on the phone while sitting on my porch. The wraparound porch I'd always dreamed of, the one where I sat curled up in a blanket many times as the rain fell in heavy sheets onto the ground and delighted my senses, the one that was surrounded by overgrown foliage that made me feel like a little girl spying on the world from her secure fort.

"Do some people just not laugh?" I asked. "I mean, are there people who don't laugh ever? People who don't have laughter inside of them? Because I don't laugh. Not ever. I can fake it well but it's only an act."

I don't remember what she said in reply. I don't think I was really meant to remember all the details of the conversation, only that bit. So that, one day, when my laughter returned, I would know I hadn't made up the memory of its absence. That I wasn't just having a bad day or a rough season; rather the light that was once in me had been so dimmed that my laughter had dried up entirely. It had so wholly disappeared I wasn't even sure anymore that I had ever laughed.

But I had.

I knew I had, because as soon as I asked the question, I remembered being a little girl who was often so overcome with laughter that it felt like I might burst into a million tiny iridescent bubbles. Then I wondered: *If you lose your laughter, can you get it back?*

Yes, you can. If you've ever wondered, as I wondered, whether a dead thing can be brought back to life, wonder no more. It can. You can. Let me be for you hopeful proof of that.

All of us feel a little lifeless inside sometimes. We all have areas of our hearts that have grown cold or apathetic. Passions that once burned white hot deep inside are now more at a Starbucks beverage post-litigation temperature. Social justice causes that once stole our sleep as we plotted righteous victory are now filed away in the "there's no hope, so I might as well take a nap" category. People we once loved, who used to get our "best hot rollers in the hair" selves, now have to make due with our "maybe there's something to that no-shampoo movement" selves.

If this describes you, don't worry. It will pass. Enjoy those naps while they last. Because soon you'll be back to the sleepless nights—whether due to passionate causes or just straight-up "down girl" variety passion.

Life is hard. We get tired. It happens. Those types of coolings are more like little hibernations. They come like the clouds that pass over us, causing us to pull our sweaters more tightly around our shoulders, then leave when the sun reemerges, coaxing us to cast off those same sweaters so that the sun may gently kiss our shoulders. Warmth returns to fill our bodies, passions reignite, causes steal our slumber once again, and we're back to searching our Sephora apps for the best hair-moisturizing treatments.

But maybe you wish that the clouds would keep the sun out of sight. Maybe you've been waiting for the sun to reemerge for so long that you've forgotten entirely what its warm kisses feel like. Maybe you feel numb, broken of heart, and so exhausted and out of fight that even the things that once made your pulse quicken and your body come alive, the things that made you want to create art in an attempt to capture even a taste of what you just experienced, seem to have forever lost their power and allure.

Perhaps even the things that do bring you joy—the warm breath of a child upon your neck, the falling rain, the perfect color of a tulip—simply wash over you, noticed and appreciated but stirring nothing deep inside as they once did. Maybe your life has become a series of days in which you go through the motions, putting one foot in front of the other, washing one dish and then another, until you crawl back into that bed you wish you'd never left to begin with.

Maybe you're like I was. Maybe you have a one thing that you're scared to look at. Maybe pretending that it doesn't exist has caused you to betray yourself over and over again that you have become numb in an effort to not feel the pain of that betrayal, to not agonize over the question of what if?

But then, what would happen if you turned and looked at that one thing—disintegrating relationship, addiction, abuse, eating disorder, self-loathing, anger at God—and said,

> Yes, you are scary. Yes, facing you will lead me into the unknown. And yes, leaping into that unknown will feel like falling into an abyss for a little while. But I am not intimidated by you anymore, because my destruction no longer awaits me at the bottom of that abyss. No, instead, there is the safety and security and love I've been nurturing as I've cultivated a life that will catch me when I fall.

Then took that leap?

As I type these last few words of this book, I still don't know what will become of my marriage. I'm still sailing through the unknown, still trying to figure it all out. I still have moments of self-doubt, and I fear that I might be headed down the wrong path. But then I look around and see the array of bright, new flourishing in my life, and I know that whatever the ending of my story may be, this path I am currently traversing is the right one.

Somehow within this long, painful scrutiny, I am finding myself again. I love who I am. I love who I'm becoming. And I love the life I am creating.

Cheered on by my children, I took one wobbly step onto

the trampoline and began to jump. Hesitantly at first, then with a little more daring. It would be so poetic to end this book by telling you that I then began to soar through the air with confidence and joy and grace. But that's not what happened. What actually happened—which will surprise you not at all—is that I instantly lost my balance and toppled over like some sort of plump drunk kangaroo.

How easy it would have been, I thought as I flailed about, if I had never climbed onto the trampoline to begin with but kept my feet safely planted on firm ground, my pride intact. Nonetheless, coaxed forth by my children, I did climb onto that trampoline. I did jump. And, yes, for a moment, it felt like I was courting death. But then all those millions of tiny woven fibers that made up the trampoline caught me and propelled me back into the air where, just for a moment, I was weightless. And free. And in that brief second of weightless freedom, I thought about all those parts of my life that are now strong and thriving. Parts that can be a place of security and comfort for me to land.

I finally understood that God didn't heal, restore, and create them just so they would cushion and help me to survive my falls. He gave them to me so that they would go one step further and propel me to rise.

So, surrounded by my funny, mischievous, effervescent children, I continued to jump and fall and repeat, until, like a phoenix from the ashes, my long-lost laughter rose out of me and took flight.

ACKNOWLEDGMENTS

My very most heartfelt thanks to the following people:

Lisa Jackson, from day one you have encouraged me, advocated for me, fought for me, laughed with me, and believed in me. Thanking you for making dreams come true that I hadn't even thought to dream.

Jenny Baumgartner, I always knew we were meant to work together. And what a delight it has been to watch how God, in his own perfect time, brought our paths together. You are an absolute treasure.

Christina Stafford, even on your darkest days, you are luminous. Thank you for being such a light to the rest of us.

Joe Fulwiler, thank you for your friendship, and also for your Twitter bio. (Please don't ever stop updating it.)

Cate Roberts, tiny but mighty, indeed. I will forever hold a special place in my heart for you.

Ally and Burt Martin, you both are the perfect illustration of how, when you least expect it, God will bring people into your life who feel as if they've been right by your side forever. Thank you for being such sweet friends.

Dr. G, there would be no Chapter One without you. Thank you.

Mountain Butorac, I had no doubt that the experience would be utterly life changing when you led our group on a pilgrimage through Italy. But I didn't expect to walk away with such a dear new friend. Thank you for all of it.

Liz Aiello, Adam Hamway, Scott Shea, Jackie Resciniti, Joe Zwilling, Tyler Veghte, and the entire Catholic Channel family, the passion and talent and fun that you all bring to the world of radio is such a joy. Thank you for welcoming me into your family so warmly. I will always treasure the memories of our time spent working together.

Charlene Balota, if everyone learned how to pour as much color and kindness into the world as you do, what an extraordinary world it would be!

Lino Rulli, Frank did it his way and so do you, and it is an utter delight to behold. Never underestimate the joy you bring into people's lives.

The Charriers, I still dream of our days and nights at Piney Point. A piece of my heart will always remain in Maryland and with you all.

Granny, not a day goes by that I don't miss your fierce, irrepressible spirit.

The Ramsdells, to have been born into this family of locusts makes me feel like the luckiest gal in all the land.

Nama and Opa, even though we are separated by the thin veil that stands between this life and the next, I still feel you both so near to me, and it brings me such comfort.

Valerie Valle and Hannah Davies, you two have always

been more like sisters to me than friends, and I am so grateful to God for the gift of you.

Mason Farnan, we miss you terribly, but we are so happy to see you leaving your unique and beautiful mark upon the world! Thank you for saving me over (and over and over) again!

Marimikel, you will always be my ittle-Lay issy-Say. I love you!

Mom, if I've said it once, I've said it a million times, but still it bears repeating: thank you for showing me how the act of savoring your passions can add love and light and a dash of magic to your entire life.

Dad, no matter what crazy choices I've made in life, no matter where they've led me, you have never failed to tell me how proud you are of me, and it's meant everything. Thank you.

Father Kyle Manno, I am prone to hyperbole, this is true. But it's no exaggeration to say that without your many prayers and endless encouragement (and patience with said tendency toward hyperbole), this book would not exist. Thank you a dozen times over.

Jen Fulwiler, SHE FLIES AT MIDNIGHT! I think that pretty much says it all, don't you?

Dan Lord, I will forever be grateful to you for creating so many captivating little creatures with me. I feel like their irresistibility speaks very highly of us, indeed.

My children, Daniel, Jack, Sophia, Lucy, Zelie, Charlie, Max, Penelope, and little Clementine (up in heaven), what wondrous, enchanting creatures you are. Being your mother is my greatest honor and never-ending delight.

NOTES

1. Hallie Lord, Facebook, November 2, 2016, https://www.facebook.com/HallieNLord/posts/1101979026587031/.
2. C. S. Lewis, *The Four Loves* (New York: HarperOne, 2017).
3. Pope John Paul II Karol Wojtyła, "A Meditation on Givenness," *Communio: International Catholic Review* 41, no. 4 (Winter 2014): 871–72, https://www.communio-icr.com/articles/view/a-meditation-on-givenness.

ABOUT THE AUTHOR

Hallie Lord is the author of *On the Other Side of Fear*, cohost of *Beatbox Gospel* podcast, cofounder of Mixi Media, and a mom of eight kids. In her free time, she can be found searching for her inner peace on Sephora .com or in the drive-through lane of the Charleston, South Carolina, Starbucks near her home. Follow her on Instagram at @HallieLord.